Having advocated *Chicken Soup for the Soul, Men are from Mars, Women are from Venus, The Answer,* and *The Secret,* it's my pleasure to encourage those readers to acquire my mentor Bernardo Moya's great work. *The Question* defines the final work of growth, asking the one right QUESTION -and now you will. . .

> *Berny Dohrmann,*
> *Chairman CEO Space International*

Question everything. This book offers a treasure map to discover anything one could want from life and business.

> *Dr. Greg Reid, author of* Stickability *and*
> *co-author of* Three feet of Gold *and*
> Thoughts are Things

The Question challenges each of us to be engaged with issues facing the world today -whatever your position may be. While thought-provoking, it is intended to highlight the way to becoming the BEST YOU possible.

> *Sharon Lechter, author of* Think and
> Grow Rich for Women, *co-author of* Think and
> Grow Rich, Three Feet from Gold,
> Outwitting the Devil *and*
> Rich Dad Poor Dad

Bernardo Moya has been a student, promoter of my work, and a friend for over a decade. This book offers *his* view of how people change for the better. This unique view pro-vides the reader a simple way to redefine their life, find more success and find purpose in living.

> *Dr. Richard Bandler, Co-creator of NLP*

Bernardo Moya's book *The Question* provides powerful, real and meaningful answers to many all-too-common modern-day dilemmas. His work with many of the world's greatest personal development gurus helps to underpin the validity of his insightful message.

If you have more questions than answers in your life, buy this book now.

Paul Boross. The Pitch Doctor

Bernardo provides a fascinating insight into how to become the best you possible in every area of your life. He gives you the tools you need to deep dive and create a ful-filling life for you and those you care about most. An exciting read that will leave you motivated and inspired!

Sara Davison, The Divorce Coach and
best-selling author of Uncoupling.

"Judge a man by his questions rather than his answers", is a famous expression from Voltaire. In his book, Bernardo Moya brings the wisdom of questions that the world needs to answer and act upon, and for all of us to explore in order to leave a legacy before we end our journey on this planet.

Mirela Sula, Founder of Global Woman Magazine
and Global Woman Club

THE
QUESTION
FIND YOUR TRUE
PURPOSE

BERNARDO MOYA

CAPSTONE
A Wiley Brand

© 2019 by Bernardo Moya.

Registered office
John Wiley & Sons Ltd, The Atrium, Southern Gate, Chichester, West Sussex,
PO19 8SQ, United Kingdom

For details of our global editorial offices, for customer services and for information about how to apply for permission to reuse the copyright material in this
book please see our website at www.wiley.com.

Wiley publishes in a variety of print and electronic formats and by print-on-
demand. Some material included with standard print versions of this book may
not be included in e-books or in print-on-demand. If this book refers to media
such as a CD or DVD that is not included in the version you purchased, you may
download this material at http://booksupport.wiley.com. For more information
about Wiley products, visit www.wiley.com.

Designations used by companies to distinguish their products are often claimed
as trademarks. All brand names and product names used in this book are trade
names, service marks, trademarks or registered trademarks of their respective
owners. The publisher is not associated with any product or vendor mentioned
in this book.

Limit of Liability/Disclaimer of Warranty: While the publisher and author have
used their best efforts in preparing this book, they make no representations or
warranties with respect to the accuracy or completeness of the contents of this
book and specifically disclaim any implied warranties of merchantability or fitness for a particular purpose. It is sold on the understanding that the publisher
is not engaged in rendering professional services and neither the publisher nor
the author shall be liable for damages arising herefrom. If professional advice
or other expert assistance is required, the services of a competent professional
should be sought.

Library of Congress Cataloging-in-Publication Data is available.

ISBN 978-0-857-08789-8 (paperback)
ISBN 978-0-857-08809-3 (ePDF)
ISBN 978-0-857-08798-0 (ePub)

Cover Design: Jason Anscomb

Set in 11/15pt and ITC New Baskerville by SPi-global, Chennai

Printed in Great Britain by TJ International Ltd, Padstow, Cornwall, UK

10 9 8 7 6 5 4 3 2 1

Contents

My Manifesto: The Way I See It

Dear friend,

What do you want out of life and how can you get it? This is The Question we all must ask ourselves if we want fulfilment, if we are looking for a meaning to our lives, if we want to be *more*. And this is The Question this book is here to help you answer.

My life so far has been interesting, challenging and exhilarating. I've worked very hard, I've lost everything, I've felt tremendous happiness and terrible fear. I've hit rockbottom many times. It's been scary, frustrating, and overwhelming at times, but it has also been exciting, fun and deeply fulfilling. I've really lived.

My pride and joy? My family, without a doubt. I've worked thousands of hours, many more than I should have, sacrificing time with my family. It's all been in pursuit of my dream to help people be the best they can be in order to live their best life.

I came to the world of personal development late in life. In my early forties I found myself in a place of despair, darkness and tremendous uncertainty, after losing everything and going bankrupt. I knew I had to start all over again and I did.

I found a book that inspired me. It triggered something in me. The book was *Change Your Life in Seven Days* by Paul McKenna. After reading it I attended a seminar called Licensed Practitioner of Neuro-Linguistic Programming with Dr Richard Bandler, one of the co-founders of the technique.

The seminar left me feeling empowered and inspired like never before, and I knew others would feel the same. I was determined to help spread this message of personal development.

Maybe something similar has happened to you. Maybe it was a seminar, a book, a quote, or something someone said to you. It gives a feeling that you are hearing the right question at the right time. It's a turning point that makes you look at your life more closely, forcing you to think about what you can do to realise your fullest potential and to help others.

At that time I was working in real estate and knew what I was doing wasn't fulfilling enough for me. I knew I needed more and I had more to give. Do you feel like that? Do you want to do more? To *be* more?

To fast-forward, for the last 10 years I have been working with Dr Richard Bandler and Paul McKenna, promoting them, supporting their methods and understanding of teaching and helping more people discover how to unlock their potential. My company, *NLP Life Training*, is now the largest NLP training company in the world.

Five years into that journey, I founded *The Best You*, a personal development platform dedicated to helping others enhance their lives through live events, EXPOs, online learning, and publications.

To say I've learned a lot is an understatement. It hasn't always been easy, but I've met some incredible people along the way. True professionals who are passionate about helping others and inspiring them to take control of their lives, to overcome and to achieve.

I want to believe that everyone starts with the best intentions. But unfortunately there are many in the personal development industry—an industry that is supposed to help others—who are in it for the wrong reasons.

- I have come across many experts who simply copy someone else

- I have come across authors, coaches, trainers, thinkers who are not congruent with their publicly stated 'beliefs' or with what they preach—many sad and angry people with massive egos.

- I have met quite a few that could do with reading their own book, memorising it and putting it into practice.

- I have attended many seminars where ultimately the only goal was to sell to the audience, to close on a large percentage of people in the room and sell the seminar's next programme.

In the industry of personal and self-development, there is unfortunately an element of what I call '**selfish development**'. Some are in it simply, as I said, for the wrong reasons. They have lost their way and it's purely about them making money.

And then there are the consumers of the books, talks and seminars. I have realised there are three primary types of these individuals:

Type 1

- Those who don't continue to grow. They learn certain things in school and life, but that is where it stops. They get on with it and really 'live' a relatively basic life. They've let go. They've given up. They are 'those who kneel'.

Type 2

- Those who try to move forward but get stuck in their insecurities; too scared of change, or taking action. They dream big things but never actually get there; they keep procrastinating. They are basically 'sitting and looking'.

Type 3

- Last but not least, those who go and make it happen. Those who are prepared to evolve, to change, to grow, to explore, to help others and who are literally willing to die attempting to become the best version of themselves in their endeavour to help and change the world. Those who are standing up, leading the way, being watched by others and admired. This book is for those people.

Which one of the three would you rather be?

One of the books and authors that has recently impacted me very positively is *Braving the Wilderness* by Brené Brown. Brené writes about standing alone as a metaphor for bravely forging your own path, which is a courage required by every entrepreneur (or any person putting themselves out there).

Before I read Brené's book, I had spent a lot of time considering my life; and her words only served to galvanise my feelings that **I would rather be alone.** And what I mean by that is. . .

I would rather be alone if that is what it takes to be true to myself.

I would rather be alone than be with people who hurt me or don't believe in me.

I would rather be alone than be surrounded by negative people or negative words.

I would rather be alone than be with people who don't believe everyone is equal.

I would rather be alone than be with someone I don't believe in.

I would rather be alone than be with people who don't believe we can make the world a better place.

The world has more ways to stay in communication with each other today than in any other time in history, yet there is a lack of connection, of real engagement in old-fashioned deep and meaningful conversations and empathy. We humans have a natural need to connect, to rely on others, to love, to feel love, and the fact is that not even 'experts' are experts in all matters. We all need help.

But here is the thing: you live once. You think you have a long time ahead, but life is short. You have less time left than you had yesterday. And it's decreasing all the time. You must make the changes that will help you get the most out of your life now.

The first thing you need to do is to be honest, honest with yourself. I discuss honesty in a later chapter. Honesty is a quality that many people struggle with. And let's be honest about being honest: if you can't be honest with yourself how can you be honest with anyone else? Which means you must STOP lying to yourself, STOP procrastinating, STOP letting others dictate your life, STOP blaming others, and face the music and deal right now with the all the things you know you need to deal with.

I believe **we are obliged** to become the best version of ourselves. Not only to benefit ourselves and those around us, but to care for the world and confront the many challenges facing humankind.

Marine biologist and explorer **Dr Sylvia Earle said**, 'You cannot care about what you do not know about.'

The fact is, if you see something wrong in the world you can either do nothing or something.

I prefer to do something. You? This book will help you focus on doing something positive rather than letting life pass you by.

I am passionate about doing what I can to make the world a better place. My pledge with all my work is to help educate, support, and create awareness on how everyone can become the best version of themselves.

Throughout my life I have had to work very hard, and although I have had an amazing team around me and the support of my family, no one in particular has gone out of their way to help me. You cannot rely on others. It is down to you to do the hard work.

I also learned many years ago that you can't please everyone all the time, and that's OK.

If you want to become the best version of yourself—The Best You; not the best copy of someone else—you must start by asking yourself important questions. This book is here to help you do that. So if you believe we have to make this amazing, beautiful world of ours a much better place to live in, let's join forces and **DO SOMETHING.**

Bronnie Ware is an Australian nurse who worked for many years in palliative care. She spent years recording the regrets of those who were nearing the end of their life and compiled them in a best-selling book, *The Top Five Regrets of the Dying*. The book listed the most common regrets as:

1. **I wish I'd had the courage to live a life true to myself, not the life others expected of me.**

   The most common regret occurs when people who recognise the end is near look back and see how many of their dreams have been unrealised.

2. **I wish I hadn't worked so hard.**

3. **I wish I'd had the courage to express my feelings.**

4. **I wish I had stayed in touch with my friends.**

5. **I wish I had let myself be happier.**

'Many did not realise until the end that happiness
is a choice,' writes Ware, of patients who had stayed
stuck in old habits. Familiarity deadened their emotions. 'Fear of change had them pretending to others,
and to their selves, that they were content, when deep
within, they longed to laugh properly and have silli-
ness in their life again.'

We must have moral responsibility and strive to do our
best to live a life without regrets.

Let me end with this: An explorer I interviewed called
Roz Savage told me that she once wrote two eulogies for
herself. The first was based on her life and her current
achievements; continuing to live as she was, not taking too
many risks.

The second eulogy was one with no regrets, doing the things
that excited her, that gave her goosebumps, and made her
feel alive. This second one is a life where, at the end of it,
you know you've lived and that you've made a difference.

This book will encourage you to be completely honest with
yourself. It will show you how to learn. How to think, to be
aware of the quality of those thoughts and to encourage
yourself to always think big. And it will teach you that it's
never too late to achieve anything you want in life. Becoming The Best You starts with YOU

And what I mean by this is to stop blaming other people,
circumstances, where you live, the economy. Start Now!
Why not?

Introduction

In my years working with and promoting the very best in the world of personal development, I have seen many people radically change for the better through self-help guidance. I've seen extraordinary transformations. People who have felt desperate and hopeless about their weight, their work, their family, or their life in general, have gone on to take powerful advice or enter a life-changing programme. I have even seen people on the brink of suicide find new meaning in life, and go on to embrace their futures with renewed hope and positivity.

It is a heartening and empowering experience watching geniuses at work—and deeply rewarding. Knowing that the work I do can connect people with empowering ideas and make their lives so much better is what keeps me going. Knowing how transformative this work can be, I am extremely happy to recommend that you read and study the greats (I name a few later). At the same time, working with and closely studying these luminaries, I have formed my own insights into success and helping people get what they want in life. I've seen what works, and I've witnessed what doesn't. That is what I'm offering here, to share with you all the powerful insights that I have built up over the last decade.

Important to note is that, when you work with so many greats it's difficult to come forward and share your story, but there comes a time in life when you need to come forward, step up, hold the flag, stand under the light.

This book in very simple terms intends to make you think, to make you think quality thoughts, to think BIG (there is no other way) and to ask yourself POSITIVE and EMPOWERING QUESTIONS. That is it in a nutshell.

I've used my experience to help me build up my business, *The Best You*. It offers a platform to showcase the techniques and advice from the world's greatest thought leaders. Techniques I've seen result in positive change. That's how I know they work.

At the same time, I'm human. I have flaws. I've made many mistakes (and still make them!), and that's another reason why I'm writing this book—so you don't have to make my mistakes and so that you can benefit from my experience.

My journey of self-discovery took a real turn in my mid-thirties. Up to then, I had experienced life at a reactive level, without really taking charge. Even so, I thought I was relatively well-read and pretty successful thanks to my skills in selling.

My early years were no different nor more challenging than many other people. I was born in London, the son of Spanish immigrants—both were very hardworking, as immigrants often are. I was later raised in Spain by my two loving parents who saw to it that I grew up happy and secure.

That changed at the age of 15, when my father died. My mum, as many widowed parents do, became 'super human,' working hard to provide for me, ensuring I had a great education, and giving me a firm understanding of the importance of hard work, respect and self-belief.

My early jobs included working in a bar as a DJ during summers and on weekends starting when I was 15 up until my mid-twenties. I also spent 13 months in the military police at the age of 19. But my first proper job came when I was 20 when I started selling timeshare properties.

I went broke twice. The first time was at the age of 26. I had a nine-month-old son and a pregnant wife at the time, and there was nothing to do but carry on. Five years later, though, I was worth millions on paper. The going was good for many years.

Then, at the age of 40, I lost it all again. This second time around was much worse. I went from living a very comfortable life in a beautiful house with money in the bank to having nothing overnight. It was terrifying. I'd wake up in the middle of the night worried, doubting myself, and unsure of how I was going to provide for my loved ones.

What I learned was I had to go back to basics, and take a day at a time.

But the second bankruptcy also brought another turning point. Things were changing. I had already started to get a new understanding of myself and the world, and this second great loss was what cleared the way for me to follow my true passion.

So, what started this transformation?

As I mentioned previously it was Paul McKenna's *Change Your Life In Seven Days,* when I became aware of Neuro-Linguistic Programming.

The book was powerful, and after taking NLP training and attending numerous seminars run by Paul McKenna in London, the extraordinary changes I saw in people at those trainings inspired me so much that I decided to help others. Back then, I also wanted to put into writing what I had begun to learn, so others could benefit from it. I became an NLP Practitioner, Master Practitioner, and eventually an NLP Trainer under the guidance of Dr Richard Bandler, co-creator of NLP.

But there was plenty more for me to do in-between times, and many more life lessons to come. They say your passion pulls you in certain directions, and I soon found that after Paul moved to America, I had the opportunity to continue running the training courses in London for Richard Bandler and at a later date Paul McKenna too.

I remember the day I made the decision to take that opportunity. I was at home, sitting with my wife in Spain, in the middle of an unfolding disaster. At the time, my real estate company was going under, and now I was being told that the option of running a training company was on the table. What should I do? There was a moment when I had to decide. Was I willing to pursue it? If I did, it meant leaving my family in Spain, commuting weekly to London and promoting events and seminars—something new that I had absolutely no idea about. I had experience in sales and marketing, but not running events and everything that is required to put them together.

Suddenly, the questions came to me: *If not me, then who? And if not now, then when?*

It was a surreal moment. With that decision I became a high-profile leader for the man I had been learning NLP from. One day I'm training with these guys, the next day I am trying to negotiate fees.

It was a huge leap. Yet, it was the right thing to do.

Ten years on, my company is one of the largest personal development organisations in the world. We train and connect with tens of thousands of people every year through our events. We hold *The Best You* EXPOs and publish one of the foremost personal development magazines with over 50,000 digital subscribers. And along the way I have had the pleasure of meeting, working with and interviewing so many great people.

I am now over 50 and if there's one thing I've learned, it's that it's vital to adapt. The NLP training company I took over has grown and changed so much in 10 years, and I've had to change along with it. I'm now also Chief Inspirational Officer of *The Best You*, a leading personal development company based in London, with a global reach. My personal experience from seeing the good that personal development can do, from seeing the extraordinary, talented people who help others find their way in the world, has inspired me to write this book.

I can't possibly list them all, but the work and books of many self-help geniuses have shaped me. Napoleon Hill, Jim Rohn, Stephen R. Covey, Tony Robbins, Les Brown, Brian Tracey, Eckhart Tolle, Jack Canfield, Bob Proctor, Robert Kiyosaki, Sharon Lechter, Richard Branson, John DeMartini, Deepak Chopra, Dr Kevin Schwartz, Jason Vale, Sir Clive Woodward, Michael Neill, Robert Holden, Grant Cardone, Barbara de Angelis, Mastin Kipp and Breneé Brown are just a few. And of course I've had the honour to work directly with John LaValle, Paul McKenna and especially Dr Richard Bandler who I am deeply grateful to.

In my personal development journey, I've been privileged to meet people who have helped bring about changes in people's lives, not only in developed countries but also in those in some of the most trying conditions in the world. I've met inspirational leaders, artists, Olympians, business-people, healers and helpers.

With all the knowledge and wisdom I've absorbed, I have come to realise I can't just keep my insights to myself. I know others will find them powerful. Useful.

Everything created in the world is originated by a question. Questioning things is good—being curious, wanting to know more, pushing yourself on.

In this book I look at the core skills of how some people push themselves and go further, while others simply give up—*live without attempting to make a dent in this planet.*

Life is a collection of memories of moments; understanding your true meaning and purpose will ensure you live a life with no regrets. A life where hopefully at the end of your days you will know you did everything in your power to truly live a fulfilled life.

So, this book is designed to encourage you to ask the same questions of yourself that the extraordinary people I've met over the years, in their different ways, have asked themselves.

The Question has many forms:

What am I here for?

What can I do to make a difference in the world?

How do I live a fulfilled, happy life?

What do I do now?

How do I make the world a better place?

That is what this book is about, and it is also about the attitude of those who have successfully answered those questions.

I believe you're a tenant on our planet and you have obligations, responsibilities.

Don't hide, don't leave it to others! Don't leave it to 'them'.

The model I'm offering in this book comes from a lifetime of experience; from pursuing the wrong ways to go as well as the right ways to go; of continual change; of fighting to survive and getting on.

Over my ten years in the personal development industry, I have met and connected with more than a hundred thousand people.

This book is dedicated to you if you want to push yourself, find out what you are capable of, so you can ultimately be THE BEST YOU CAN BE.

No excuses, no bullshit. Just keep going and be relentless in your quest.

You can refer my web page www.bernardo-moya.com and the books web page (now live) www.thequestion.co for further information.

Chapter 1

HOW ARE WE?

A Quick Review: Current State of Affairs

Earth is 4.54 billion years old, within an error range of 50 million years.

According to the Population Reference Bureau, since then an estimated 107 billion people in total have lived on our planet. Just a tiny proportion of those has made a truly global impact by providing the world with new technology, transportation, medicine, education, or in other ways that have made the world a better place. I am aware that not everyone can make a global impact or has the urge to, and being a great parent, an inspiring teacher or a doctor makes the world a better place. . .

I am simply exploring how many out of the 107 billion could have done more, been more, seen more, achieved more, contributed more; how many of those, rich and wealthy, poor and unfortunate, could have made the world a better place, but left this world with deep regrets?

All over the world, people are hoping, seeking, working and praying for better lives.

In today's super-connected world, more people than ever have the chance to make positive change. All over the world, people see what they have now and dream of ways to improve their lives. In the poorest parts of the world they might be seeking stability, food for their families, security and a place to live. A place where they can feel anchored, to grow and to realise their full potential.

And that story isn't just true of people in poorer places. Though it's on a different scale and with different challenges, that's pretty much what everyone everywhere wants.

There are vast differences in wealth across the world. The issue of wealth and income inequality is one of the great moral issues of our time; it is certainly the great economic issue of our time. It is estimated that 1 per cent of the world's population controls more wealth than the remaining 99 per cent combined, according to financial institution Credit Suisse.

We live in a world where the vast majority have to work very hard to make a living. That probably includes you.

Your religion, race, sex and country of origin can all massively impact your ability to succeed or to find places to succeed. For centuries, countries have been building imaginary borders walls and fences that in some cases make success for the masses harder. Today, some countries and continents have strict immigration laws; we seem to be going back to more segregation and less integration.

But it must not continue that way. Here's why.

Change is Coming

In large part due to technology.

Because of technology, more people are engaging with the wider world, acting, reacting, coming forward, doing, rebelling, exploring. Every telephone mast, every new phone line or wireless connection allows someone new to come into this amazing 'future' that a lot of us are already living in.

In 1995 only 0.4 per cent of the population had access to the internet. Only the most visionary people had an inkling of how profoundly it would change people's lives in the years to come. Now, the internet is accessible to more than 49.2 per cent of the population—that's more than 3.6 billion people. This is already having a massive, positive impact all over the world.

I believe that this huge change will allow something even more positive to happen. It will allow hope to flourish.

I am a firm believer that communication is the great hope for mankind. Communication is the great skill humans have above all other animals. Language is precise and nuanced in humans in a way that no other creature can match. It allows us to know each other and understand each other.

The great hope I have for technology is that it allows more people to communicate, become more open, more integrated and have more love for others. Indeed, right now, knowledge, ideas and wisdom are being shared through the world wide web. Go on YouTube and you can learn anything from making a *crème brulée* to building a motorbike engine—or of course, you can watch a cat playing a piano, or doing something else that is equally funny!

What does this mean?

The World is Open for Business in More Ways than Ever Before

Despite the walls and fences that in some places are going up anew, in many ways the world is more open than it ever has been. It's more open for business, for learning, for understanding.

Thanks to phone apps, computer programs and the hardware that supports them, start-up businesses are having an instant and massive impact. Thanks to social media, people are prepared to push the boundaries, question established wisdom, learn what seemed impossible, invent, push further, break records and create new paradigms.

We are at the start of a new leap forward for humanity, the result of a building momentum since the start of the Industrial Revolution more than 200 years ago. In the last 100 years, the momentum has really increased spectacularly. We've had amazing breakthroughs.

Just over 100 years ago in 1903, the Wright brothers' first aeroplane, the Wright Flyer, skipped into the air from a field near Kitty Hawk, North Carolina. It was the start of a whole new journey for humanity, with increased communication and ever easier travel. Just 66 years later in 1969, men stood on the moon. Two years after the Russians had sent an unsuccessful rover to Mars, in 1997, the new generation of rovers began rolling across the red planet. That's less than 100 years from the first successful powered flight! Now plans are underway to send people to Mars by 2030.

On Earth, a new breed of tech pioneers has established brands with global recognition. Apple, Amazon, Uber, Skype, Spotify, YouTube, Google, Airbnb, Microsoft, Hewlett-Packard, Netflix—the list goes on—are now part of our everyday lives. Meanwhile Tesla, Virgin Galactic, Reaction Engines, SpaceX, Sierra Nevada and many others are at the same stage as the generation of aviators were who came after the Wright brothers over 100 years ago—getting ready to take humankind further than ever before.

In technology, another growing area of change and expansion is artificial intelligence (AI), in which computers learn how to learn so that they can make their own decisions. The menial and not-so-menial jobs of the past, such as driving, warehousing and even clerical jobs, are being automated.

It's an extraordinary time of change, renewal, vigour and growth that will also mean upheaval, dislocation and revolution. We all need to be ready for that change and to make the most of it. Now more than ever there are opportunities for human beings to release their potential and no longer be caught in the everyday humdrum life of the world. But with these technological advances comes the danger of many people being left behind, of a tech-poor class being ruled over by a tech-rich elite.

Our Past

In order to understand where we are going, we have to remember where we came from. We have to appreciate what our ancestors had to go through to allow us to live how we live today with the freedoms we enjoy. But most importantly, we should learn from their mistakes and from our own.

We are living in an extraordinary time. Never before has there been so much opportunity and so much danger for the human race all at once. Yet, if you have an optimistic view of the world like me, your focus will be on the opportunity this amazing world offers.

The great philanthropic entrepreneur and inventor Elon Musk said:

'If anyone thinks they'd rather be in a different part of history, they're probably not a very good student of history. Life sucked in the old days. People knew very little and you were likely to die at a young age of some horrible disease. You'd probably have no teeth by now. It would be particularly awful if you were a woman.'

In those 4.5 billion years, *Homo sapiens* has only been around for a tiny fraction of that time. It has been an incredible journey for humanity, which has travelled at breakneck speed to a position of dominance on the planet.

Louise Leakey, granddaughter of the famous anthropologist Louis Leakey, explains in a TED talk she gave:

'If there are 400 sheets of tissue paper in the roll, then the very first life in the oceans is seen at sheet 240. The age of the dinosaurs begins at sheet 19. Dinosaurs in their many forms and great diversity are around for 14 and a half sheets. Dinosaurs are extinct by the end of the Cretaceous, 5 squares from the end, making way for the mammals.

'Our story and place on the timeline as upright walking apes begins only in the last half of the very last sheet. The human story as *Homo sapiens* is represented by less than 2 millimeters of this, some 200,000 years.'

Though that number of 107 billion people in total having lived since the very start of the human race may seem like a lot, if you think that right now there are around 7.4 billion on the planet, expected to be 9 billion by 2050 and 11.2 billion by 2100, then the achievements of the 'few' who came before us have been extraordinary.

What's more, though *Homo sapiens* emerged around 200,000 years ago, civilisation is a relatively new idea. The first cities were built around 6,000 years ago. That's only 200 generations from then to now. In the intervening 60 centuries, so much has happened, so many great cultures have risen and fallen, so many people have lived, loved and built what we take for granted today.

Even the idea of civilisation has come a long way. One of the newest flourishings of thought is the increasing rise of the non-religious mind.

The religious mind has changed, too. Sacrifice, let alone human sacrifice, is no longer part of everyday society. Yet many cultures we look back on in awe practised sacrificial offerings as a part of their religious beliefs. The Aztecs, Etruscans, Egyptians, Romans and Incas sacrificed humans and animals. Though many people were drugged and sacrificed against their will, others were sold a priestly lie about an eternity in heaven and then offered themselves freely.

At first it sounds like a joke to imagine the modern-day teen preparing himself for sacrifice. Can you imagine two kids today saying: 'Hey, are you coming to see a movie this afternoon?' and the other replying: 'No, can't do it. I'm sacrificing myself. I'm going to heaven this afternoon.'

But vestiges of outmoded ways of thinking do still exist. These days, human sacrifice is performed by members of insurgent groups, not mainstream religions; it's done not with knives in a temple, but with an explosive belt in a marketplace. Such tragedies show us, in many ways, how short a time it is since the days of deep superstition.

Though modern civilisation is sometimes brutal, there's no doubt our ancestors were more brutal. Depending on their culture, they were highly creative in thinking up new ways of killing or torturing. You name it, it's been done.

Some of the reasons for all that killing, torture and death can only be thought of as absurd.

In the period of the Spanish Inquisition, an *auto-da-fé* saw people tortured and burned alive just for thinking differently from the priests who held power over them. In South America, Spanish colonists deemed it acceptable to kill natives because they *didn't have souls.*

The British Empire degraded, massacred and raped its way across much of the known world, destroying local economies and making them dependent on Britain as their hub. Most other European nations did something similar, using more or less brutality to achieve their goals.

In the 20th century, political ideologies were the killers.

Tens of millions died in Stalin's Communist Purges, with quotas for executions plucked from thin air and massacres arranged with the stroke of a pen.

Under the Maoist regime in China, it is estimated 80 million people died as a result of the Cultural Revolution.

Hitler's regime murdered 11 million noncombatants and desecrated their bodies. Six million of those were Jewish. Others had mental health issues, were of supposedly 'poor' genetic stock, or did not fit in with the Nazi's Aryan 'master race.'

Capitalism has been the driver for amazing advances in technology, medicines and culture, and has simultaneously ensured that inequality is built into everyone's lives. Billions of people have died because they cannot get the medicines and food they require, the clean water they need or the freedom from strife they crave, due to the inherent instability and unfairness at the heart of capitalism, even though there is actually plenty for everyone.

In the modern day, new dangers have risen. Humans have become so dominant as a species that we threaten many other species on the planet through deforestation, over-hunting, climate change, plastic pollution and nuclear disaster, to name a few pressing problems.

And yet. . . and yet I remain an optimist—and optimism is at the heart of the traits you need to make your life better. I believe we can evolve to be better than we are. I believe we can learn the lessons of the past, and build a new and better world that obliterates the cruelty and madness that came before.

Why do I believe this? Because there is something extraordinary about humanity and that includes you.

Look at the evidence. Over millennia, men and women have travelled looking for food, for new ways to live, to escape captivity, to survive and sometimes to conquer others. Men and women have traversed continents; migratory wave after wave has walked, ridden on horseback, sailed in boats, crossed seas and oceans looking for a better life, for wealth, or hoping to bring their version of truth to the world.

Look at human achievement. The designing and building of impressive bridges that span seas and rivers; tunnels in the most impossible places; pyramids; cathedrals; and the most amazing buildings and structures were all made using rudimentary tools and equipment, often taking centuries to complete.

I want us to turn on our senses and really try and visualise what it might have been like in a different time from now. I want you to see what you would see, hear what you would hear and feel what you would feel if you were present at the following scenarios.

Let's imagine some different scenarios.

Let's Imagine—1

For a moment, let's put ourselves in the shoes of those who went before.

How do the lives of the people involved in those ancient endeavours compare to yours? What was their journey long before you were born? What does it tell us about ourselves?

I invite you to imagine it was you in the place of your ancestor.

People have been setting out in handcrafted boats crossing vast oceans for thousands of years. Four thousand years ago, merchants set out from the shores of Egypt to trade with a massive network of tribes that stretched from the shores of the Levant to the southern coast of Spain, all the way across the treacherous Bay of Biscay, to the shores of Northern England and finally across to Scandinavia, where they traded for amber. The Vikings set out regularly across the North Atlantic to trade in Iceland and Greenland, as well as to pillage Europe. Traces of Viking archaeological remains have even been found far, far away from Scandinavia in North America! The people of Easter Island are related to those of South America—meaning that at some point thousands of years ago, Native South Americans set sail on reed boats and plotted by sun and star to arrive thousands of miles away on a tiny rock in the Pacific.

Imagine yourself as one of these travellers, climbing into an open boat or very small ship with little cover and protection from the rain and the sun. Maybe you are a slave, forced to row when the wind dies down. Perhaps you have never been on the water before and you see the dark depths heaving around you, with giant fish and sharks circling. You feel the gruelling routine every day, your hands grip the oars as the wind dies and you experience desperate days on end when you are becalmed. Your water supply begins to fail you, filthy water green with scum is splashing in a thin film at the bottom of the water skins. The crew draws lots to decide who will be eaten when the food runs out. The searing heat of the sun burns into your head and others grow weak and sick.

But then the weather breaks and rainwater floods down. The revivifying water slakes your thirst and gives you hope and, as you are blown forward, the shout comes up: 'Land! Land!' You heave a sigh of relief. You've made it! You're going to live.

When our ancestors crossed the oceans, the hardships they faced were many and various. They faced annihilation at the hands of a cruel natural world, protected only by the sides of the vessel and the determination to go on, no matter what.

These are the amazing lives of the people who went before us. Many of our extraordinary predecessors would have faced even greater hardships when they crossed oceans and seas for the first time. Our modern troubles, at least for many in the West, are small in comparison.

Yet though we are heirs to the impressive achievements of those who went before us, every generation has its heroes, its survivors and those who have moved civilisation forward.

Let's Imagine—2

Four and a half thousand years ago in ancient Egypt the state religion had such a powerful message that it inspired the Pharaoh Khufu to order a massive monument built to protect his mortal remains and ensure that his soul lived on into eternity. It was to be a project on a massive scale. The idea of pyramids had been around for thousands of years, from the ancient low-walled *mastabas* still found in desert complexes to grand masses of stone that would last forever. Khufu's idea was that he would build the grandest ever pyramid—a man-made mountain in the sands.

Khufu deployed tens of thousands of slaves to quarry and move massive stones, many weighing 50 tons or more, through the hot sands—all for a religious idea! Those slaves toiled and sweated and died in the sands. They had no mechanised lifting equipment. Brute manpower, wet sand to slide the blocks on and leverage were the tools of the day. How many were crushed to death? How many lost limbs? Yet, our ancestors rose to the task. It was the seeing through of a vision that stemmed from the imagination of the pharaoh and his priests to create something truly extraordinary. The lives of the masons working on the quarried stone were gruelling: breaking and shaping it with the most basic tools, their lungs and eyes and noses filled with dust and flies. Working day after day as the Nile floods rose and receded each year was incredibly tough. And yet one of them could easily be one of your ancestors. As could the foremen overseeing the project or the slaves who toiled and sweated and died in the sands. They pushed on and created and laboured and made something that the world to this day, four and a half millennia on, still marvels at.

The pyramids have survived for thousands of years.

And every single thing that has been created in the world started in someone's mind.

People can achieve great things, if only they know what great things to achieve. Perhaps they can create something more useful than a man-made mountain, if only they have the right vision!

Let's Imagine—3

In Europe, millennia later, think of the soldiers of the Roman Empire, who often had to leave their families and loved ones for journeys to new frontiers where they would campaign, fight and face death on a daily basis.

Imagine it's you. You have two young kids and a beautiful wife. Because you are a soldier you are forced to leave your hometown and follow your general on his journey to conquer new lands. Your feet are wrapped in furs in the cold, and in lighter boots and sandals in the dry weather, but are calloused and bleeding by the unending marching. It might take you years to get to your destination as you march to places no Romans have been before, facing hostile tribes, terrible weather, diseases that spread through the legions, freezing winters, burning summers, lice and fleas.

When you arrive, you know you have to kill to stay alive. Every day, fellow soldiers die around you. You are surrounded by uncertainty, you're homesick, you're scared, you're surrounded by brutality and possible death. You never know if you are going to get back home.

It's a hard life, but it's equally difficult for this Roman legionary's wife. Imagine experiencing her life. You have to get by, find work in the local markets or in the fields, look after the kids while you wait as the days, weeks, months and years go by, not knowing what has become of your loved one and realising you may never know.

Let's Imagine—4

The California Gold Rush saw the expansion of a massive population into the west of America in search of gold. Some 300,000 people flooded into California in a few short years, firstly from Oregon, Hawaii and Latin America, then in an increasing tide from across the world. Many crossed the vast plains of America in covered wagons, encountering rightly hostile native Americans protecting their ancestral lands. Many died on the way from disease or from arguments with rivals, and yet others struggled and toiled to find gold, while others gave up and perhaps more cannily decided to provide the gold hunters with supplies in the newly growing towns. It was an extraordinary time. It saw rivalries lead to murders, while other lives were transformed in the incredible press of people and commerce that founded the newly born state. It brought disastrous displacement for the Native Americans and riches to the country as a whole. It's not an easy tale to tell with a simple moral, but it's worth remembering the energy and drive that made this moment so important in so many ways.

Let's Imagine—5

Let's imagine the inventors who first dreamed of flying. From the storytellers in ancient Greece who fabricated tales of Icarus building himself wings from wax and feathers and plunging to the earth, to the book *The First Men In The Moon* by H. G. Wells, people have dreamed of soaring above the ground, even the world.

With balloon flight in France in the 18th century man experimented with lighter-than-air transport, while others dreamed of flying like a bird. Experiments in balloon flights led to explosions in the air, terrible disasters that rained fire down on the spectators below. Some balloon expeditions saw explorers attempt to fly over the North Pole—only to end in disaster, starvation or being eaten by wild creatures.

In 1799, Englishman Sir George Cayley devised the concept of the modern aeroplane. He envisaged his fixed-wing flying machine with systems for lift, propulsion and control. He designed the first reliable glider that could lift a man and predicted that the only way an aircraft could be designed would be when a small enough engine could be fixed to it.

In 1903, inspired by Cayley, the Wright brothers created the Wright Flyer, after years of study and as the technology of building a light enough engine finally caught up with Cayley's vision. From that first powered heavier-than-air flight, within 50 years humanity had broken the sound barrier. Within another 25 years it had travelled to space and the moon. Space probes are exploring beyond the edge of the solar system even now. What a short journey it has been to get this far!

And now things are accelerating. Which means things can also get better for people quicker if we just apply our minds.

In the World, Now

Down on the surface of the earth, men and women are doing more than they ever could before. An incredible struggle to do better is exemplified in sport. Olympians train for up to 8 hours every single day for years to achieve, to perfect, to move onwards and beat the records of those who went before.

Climbers have scaled the highest mountains with the most basic clothes and gear. Athletes have swum rivers and seas just to test their resistance and capabilities.

Men and women who have lost limbs now have more opportunities than ever before. Many are free to get on with their lives in ways their predecessors could never have imagined—not *disabled*, but *enabled* by society. And because of their achievements they are able to spread word of their causes to help others more effectively. Some have gone on to swim, run and cycle for charities, cross seas or trek to the North and South Poles to create awareness for their causes and the charities they support.

We are all raised up and inspired by these individuals. They are beacons for us to be guided by and they are useful reality checks to help us get our own struggles in perspective.

Yet, achievement isn't only about doing. Sometimes achievement is about survival itself; about resilience and hanging on in the face of the worst odds. Humans have done terrible things to each other. They have cheated and killed others to take control of their possessions, their land and their families, or simply to have a world without them in it. Whole countries have gone to war for the sake of very stupid ideas that somehow turned out to be deeply addictive and irresistible. Men have created weapons of mass destruction. We have wiped out or attempted to wipe out complete races in acts of what are euphemistically called 'ethnic cleansing'.

That also is unfortunately part of our story.

Let's Imagine—6

Imagine yourself living not so along ago, during a period of conflict, when World War II is raging. You're living in Nazi-controlled territory, under occupation by a cruel army that has only hatred for you in its heart.

What is it like to be a kid in the midst of all that? Scared, alone, hungry and suffering daily air raids. Maybe your father is a soldier, maybe he has already died.

Imagine spending your days in a concentration camp, knowing that each day might be your last. Or imagine being a soldier on the other side, having to follow orders or risk being shot— obeying something you don't believe in, but knowing that you, your family and loved ones have got to survive somehow, and that depends on your obedience.

Then imagine being one of the liberators. You are only 18 or 19, leaping from a boat on to a beach exploding with shells and the air thick with bullets. People around you are shot and dying, yet somehow you push on. How scared you are.

We don't even have to imagine some of this horror. You can see it this very day. It is going on right now, with people fleeing war-torn regions and taking to the waters in the flimsiest of boats to find a place where they can be safe. Many drown along the way. That we have not done enough to help them is to our lasting shame.

As uncomfortable as this may be, this is humanity. It has happened and is happening to people like you and me. And yet, the good news is that there are people helping others, giving them food, clothing, housing and safety.

And on another level, if you think about all that horror and death that has gone before, then it's undeniable that you are from a line of survivors. You are the current expression of the ability to survive. It's what you and the rest of the world has in common.

But wait. Is that a selfish thought? Too selfish?
Maybe.

I remember reading Victor Frankl's book *Man's Search For Meaning,* which is based on his true story of surviving the Holocaust. In it, he describes how he lived through the awful, life-destroying conditions of a concentration camp. One thing that struck me was how he said he had to become completely *apathetic* in order to survive. Frankl confessed that apathy enabled him to shut down his emotions and stop being worn out by the horror he was seeing. All his energy was focused on his own survival. For him, that was the strategy of resilience he adopted to get by.

There's an irony here. By listening to Frankl, by using our empathy, we can learn that some people in some situations survive through apathy. The big lesson is that, at different times, you've got to know how to ask yourself the right questions and the questions change with the context. If he'd shown too much empathy at that point in his life, it's quite possible Frankl would have died. He needed to preserve his energy, to look after himself. All the finer, selfless feelings had fallen away due to the extreme position he found himself in. Frankl was an empathetic, kind writer and person, but in this context he needed to be someone quite different from his usual self. He instinctively found a survival strategy.

So, yes, it is selfish to say we all come from a line of survivors. But there are times when an interpretation, a response, is what saves you. This, too, is the skill of survival.

* * *

The Power of the Right Question

Now, think about all these stories above. Have you realised how fortunate you are?

Most people reading this book are hopefully not posted in hostile territory, are free to explore, to express themselves, to live with the extraordinary fruits of the innovators who came before them.

Realising that you are lucky is not a question of someone waving their finger at you and telling you to buck up your ideas. Instead, knowing you are in a time and place in the world where there is so much opportunity available to you thanks to those who came before—that is a realisation that will give you the power to get on in life.

It's a question that should come back to you time and again when the chips are down. It's a truly empowering question.

How lucky are you? Just how lucky?

* * *

QUESTION:
How did human beings who wanted to go further, go faster, do new things, invent, fly, go into space and break the barriers to what seemed impossible?

ANSWER:

By asking themselves—ourselves—the right questions.

* * *

Fast and Easy

We live in a world where many companies, organisations and individuals are simply interested in making a quick buck, and not really interested in who they leave behind, or use, or who gets in the way.

Right now, oil companies are destroying the environment. It's not only a question of global warming, which some people still argue isn't real, even in the face of overwhelming evidence. There are also the oil slicks, the oil rig leaks, the tankers that collide, the diesel that fills the air with poisons, the ruthless squeezing of the very last vestiges of fossil fuels from rocks by pumping sulphuric acid into the earth and into the water supplies that sustain us.

Plastic companies are polluting the seas with waste they say is not their problem. Massive multinationals use plastic on a daily basis, not caring or taking responsibility, as micro-plastics get into the most basic organisms and vast islands of plastic fill the seas, killing underwater life and affecting the plankton that produces oxygen.

Pharmaceutical companies and cartels are selling drugs. Many of the 'legal ones' you can buy over the counter have massive side effects and many of the 'illegal ones' are creating addiction. Farmers are overusing antibiotics as growth aids to increase their profits, creating superbugs for which there is no known cure.

Criminals are trafficking people through massive slave trade organisations. Slavery is now the third biggest illegal activity on earth in economic terms, after illegal drugs and counterfeiting. At the same time, speculators are destroying vast swathes of forests and poisoning rivers with mercury and other heavy metals, making the indigenous people homeless or dependent on non-sustainable modes of life, while also destroying local cultures and local wisdom. In fact, making more slaves.

This mentality doesn't care about the effects of what it does, nor in what sphere it operates. It is the activity that comes from a lack of ethics, a lack of seeking to care and nurture those around it, and profiting at the expense of others because it is fast and easy to do so.

The fast and easy is everywhere. I have seen it in the personal development industry. Although the purpose of personal development should be to empower others, so many create programmes that promise you will get rich quick. They are not interested in helping others, but have their values inverted. *Who can sell more? Who can close more deals?* These are the wrong questions. They entice people to treat others like lambs being led to the slaughter. The same thing applies to trainers and authors who copy each other and don't give credit where credit is due.

There are many, many great people in the personal development world who do beautiful and positive things. And then there are the others. The ones whom I believe are not involved in self-development, but are in the 'selfish development' business, encourage others to take without considering the consequences, or to serve themselves and their financial objectives.

It's a mentality that is going to harm us all.

Your Questions

Thankfully, it doesn't have to be like that. No one, no individual or organisation, should get away with it. Am I being unrealistic? Utopian? Maybe. But if we don't do *something*, your children's children won't have a planet to live on, or will live on a planet ruled by ruthless individuals and organisations, even more so than today.

If you can learn only one thing from this book (and I hope you can learn a lot), it is that you not only start asking yourself questions. . . you ask **The Right Ones.**

I hope this book, *The Question*, will inspire you to make use of all the extraordinary positive skills around you. That it will become a forum for 'doers', for people who care and are driven to get on with what they want to do and become who they want to be in a way that helps others to do the same.

I hope you can make an impact in some positive way to change the world around you. Of course, not everyone will become an inspirational speaker or a best-selling author. But you can be one to make an impact, starting from the bottom up, with loved ones, family, friends, colleagues and people at work, and then with their circle of people, to make the world a better place.

Such a movement starts from within. It starts with you.

So, I ask you to genuinely consider The Question: **what are you here for?**

Take a few minutes now to consider your answers to the following:

What do you want in your life?

What do you want for others?

Do you ever ask yourself these questions?

How much time do you dedicate to thinking about these questions?

What do you want to get from this book?

What did you get up for today?

Who needs you?

What are your plans?

What do you really want to do?

What are the excuses you make for not making these things happen?

Do you think it's too late? If so how do you know?

Are you thinking now's not the right time? When would be the right time? Do you have the time, i.e. are you going to be around at that later right time?

Maybe you think you haven't got the money to change your life. Do you think everyone that started a business had all the right circumstances to make things happen?

Maybe you believe your parents won't let you.

Maybe you think you are too fat, too short, too tall, too Hispanic, too black, too white. How did you come to that conclusion?

Maybe you think it's not your problem.

Maybe you think *they will sort it out?* Who are *they?*

Maybe you just don't care. Maybe you have secretly given up.

Do you tell yourself these things? If so, remember: one day your life will be over. But there might be enough time still to do what you want if you stop listening to your excuses.

Excuses will hold you back and drown you in inertia if you let them win.

If you carry on thinking them, at the end of your life you will look back on a list of regrets.

This could be a real possibility. Think about it.

* * *

QUESTION:
What do you want to achieve; what do you want to have seen, felt, touched, tasted, understood and experienced before you die? It's funny because we know we are mortals yet we believe we will live forever. For some reason we tend

to believe death will come at a convenient time and only when we have fulfilled our dreams.

Think about this. Take some time to answer now. When you've done so, write down your answers. Start a notebook and allow those answers to guide your life.

Remember: the quality of your life will depend on the quality of the questions you ask yourself.

The power of questions lies in the transformative answers they provoke. A hostile TV show interviewer can do this by setting an agenda through the power of their questions that make it difficult for the interviewee to express their message and direction.

But you don't need to do this to yourself and trip yourself up. You only need to think carefully about your honest answers to some important questions.

* * *

The Question:

What stops you? Are you hiding behind beliefs that express themselves as disempowering questions? Do you ask yourself any of these questions that hold you back?

Why I am so lazy?

Why can't I lose weight?

Why can't I find love?

Why do people take advantage of me?

Why didn't I study back when I could?

Why does no one like me?

How cold will it be today?

How busy are the roads going to be?

How much trouble will I get into this month?

Why do I have so many problems?

Why doesn't anyone help me?

Do I care? Am I really bothered about people liking me or meeting other people's stereotypes?

If so, stop it. Let this be the last day. Become aware of your internal dialogue and of your questions, and ask better ones. How we speak to ourselves is of great importance. Be aware.

* * *

Think about a simple question like 'Why can't I lose weight?' (You can change the *weight* question to be about anything).

This unhelpful question presupposes:

1. You are carrying too much weight

2. You need to lose weight

3. You aren't able to lose weight.

If you don't challenge these types of questions, you will reinforce their meaning.

If you answer with the word 'because,' then you are acknowledging the 'truth' of the question's presuppositions.

Yet, if someone was to say to you directly, 'You are too fat, you need to lose weight, but you aren't able to lose weight,' you'd probably say, 'F**k you.'

This weaselly way of asking a question creates a mind-set you wouldn't normally accept. It means you need to ask yourself the right questions—the ones that will produce the useful answers that you can do something useful with.

* * *

Questions that empower you:

'Am I really overweight?'

'Do I need to lose weight, and what would happen if I didn't? What will happen if I do?'

'Is losing weight important to me? If so, why?'

'Do I know how to lose weight?'

'Do I care that I am overweight?'

'What ways have I tried that didn't work, and how do I find ways that will work?'

* * *

Think about how empowering those questions are and notice how they start to challenge your presuppositions.

Try the same with, 'Why doesn't anybody like me?'

Ask yourself:

'Is it *really* true that nobody likes me?'

'How do I know no one likes me?

'Do I really want the specific people that I think don't like me to like me?'

'What would they bring to my life?'

Is important to me if they don't like me? And if it is, why?

And if it is, how do I know?

'What makes me want them to like me?'

'How do I go about making myself more popular?'

'What have I tried already?'

'Now, being honest with myself: what do I need to do differently?'

'Actually, are these people worth it?'

These, again, are empowering questions.

This is why it's so important to focus on questions. If you don't ask the right questions, you will always get the wrong answers.

I will say this here again and repeat it throughout the book:

The quality of your life will be based on the quality of the questions you ask yourself. And that's before you even look at the answers.

Those who never give up, who do not accept average, who work hard, who focus, who learn, who always look for the answers—the right answers—ask questions of a different sort.

Below are some better questions that people with everyday challenges can ask themselves. See which ones apply to you. And ask yourself, *are there even better questions I can ask? What are they?*

How can I become more active?

How much better can I feel today?

How am I going to lose weight? By when am I going to lose weight?

How many people would LOVE to be with me? How sexy am I?

How can I deal wisely with those who hurt me?

What can I learn today?

Where can I find like-minded people?

How lovely will life be today?

What can I read on my commute to work?

What other great ideas do I have?

What am I passionate about?

How can I serve others?

How much do I care about myself? Others? About being loved?

What do I LOVE doing?

Remember:

If you ask questions that hold you back, you will be held back.

If you think average thoughts, you will be average.

To achieve greatness, think great things.

* * *

'It always seems impossible until it's done.'
—Nelson Mandela

Believe in what you are setting out to do.

Ask the questions that will get you there.

* * *

So, is personal development, professional growth, and getting on in the world and taking charge of your life really so simple?

In many ways, yes, it is. If you start becoming aware of your internal dialogue, that voice inside your head and (for those who are questioning if you have a voice or not—that one, that's the one I am referring to) then you get the chance to control it; **to take it in the direction you want to go and to make a whole new reality and consciousness with it.**

How do you do this?

The first step is to become aware of your inner voice. What you say to yourself is of extreme importance. But it's not all internal.

It's also vital to surround yourself with positive, loving people. Ditch the bad voices and questions and the negative people in your life. Do it soon, no looking back, no regrets. You have a choice: —**it's up to you to** spend all your life trying to change those who are having a negative effect on you, or to become the person you want to be at a distance from their negative influence. Changing yourself is easier than changing others.

So start asking those empowering questions that will get you thinking in the right direction:

What are you here for?

What are you here for personally?

What are you here for professionally?

What are you here for globally?

We are only getting started. My job is to coach you. To make you think. To help you find your meaning, your passion, your mission in life.

The questions you start to ask yourself as you read this book, and over the coming days and months, are best when designed to steal the agenda away from that voice that once controlled your direction. You don't need more of the same. You need more of what will make you 'jump out of bed in the morning' like when you were a kid, remember?

We Need a New Approach!

You agree, don't you? (See what I did there?)

The first thing to remember is that we will stay on track and won't be deterred.

I believe we should use a combination of a steadily applied optimism and positive attitude— of doing what's right locally to influence what's happening globally—to make things change. Being ready to act and getting your own head in gear can make that happen. Aligning your needs and your desires with what's good for all of us, so that you don't live in a vacuum separated from others, is part of that journey.

Though you are one person, you *can* make a difference, but it's through combining many of us that we can *all together* make a massive difference.

I believe personal development is the way to free up so much potential in the world and make the world a better, a happier place.

And I think we can all agree, we need that!

I've spent many years working in the personal and professional growth industry because it's my passion. I'll share with you more about my journey in the next chapter. For now, it will be helpful for you to know that I am one of a large disparate group of people wanting to help others become the best versions of themselves. There are many of us, many people who help millions around the world.

I've been in the personal development business since 2006. I've read so many books, attended countless seminars, interviewed and studied with so many great people; and now I feel a new approach is needed.

That's why I created my company, **The Best You**. I meet with successful people and interview them for broadcast on **The Best You TV** programme and print their interviews in **The Best You Magazine** so the word can get out about what the most extraordinary and talented people do in the world today. That's also why I organise **The Best You Expos** in Europe and America—to give people the chance to connect up with each other. To enable people who really want to help others to share platforms and ideas. Because who knows what greatness and positivity can come from that?

It's said that in the world of personal development there is a lot of 'personal shelf-development' going on. People buy books and attend seminars, but then leave the books and ideas on their shelves, or take really important notes and then leave them hidden in a drawer. Does this sound familiar?

My mission with *The Question* is to really help you think, to help you find your deep passion and then hold on to it. It's simple, its straightforward, no seven steps or 22 steps, no acronyms.

It can be summarised in the words: *The Best You – A Better World.*

Let's stay positive. Does being negative help? Does worrying help? The answer is No.

With self-development we can at least take charge of our lives; to have the tools to live fuller and happier lives with more meaning and get that message out to as many people as we can.

* * *

The Question is: What is your true purpose in life?

* * *

Stan Lee, my hero and the creator of Spider-Man, said through Peter Parker's uncle, 'With great power comes great responsibility.' Whereas in Mark Manson's book *The Subtle Art of Not Giving a F*ck,* he states that with 'great responsibility comes great power.'

You, me, us. We all have the power. . .

I believe you hold a great responsibility to find your true purpose. As a fellow dweller on our planet, you have obligations to the world and everyone in it.

You're not alone. Billions and billions have come before you and risen to the challenge by answering their version of The Question.

It's worth looking at just how far we've all come and how amazing you, we, and those who went before us, really are.

My Struggles and Discoveries

I've asked myself many empowering and disempowering questions over the years. It's only lately that I've really come to understand the choices I was making—when I was just reacting and when I was really taking charge of my own path.

This book is not about my life in particular, far from it. It's about your life. It's about all our lives. But let me tell you a little more about me so you know who I am and what I've struggled with and learned. It might give you a shortcut to moving forward on your own path.

Let me be clear: My life has not been more challenging than that of millions or billions of other people all over the world. In truth, I consider myself blessed and lucky in so many ways. It's also true that everyone has struggled in their lives. What's important is to learn from people who have faced and beaten their struggles, no matter what the causes.

There's no doubt some people find a way to deal with the knocks far quicker than others. Listening to how other people deal with their own struggles can help you face your own.

Who am I? To be honest, I have been working on the 'who' for most of my life and only now is it coming into focus. The ongoing *Project Bernardo* started 53 years ago and continues today. I'm more interested than ever in learning and developing. I'm 53 but I have the curiosity and energy of a 26-year-old.

I have been an entrepreneur for more than 32 years. I have been a husband for over 30 years to my wife Julia. I have been a parent for 27 years and now am a father of three: two sons, Max and Lucci, and my daughter, Gigi.

I would describe myself as honest and loyal, as very motivated and driven, and as one who creates his own path and vision.

Both my parents were Spanish immigrants who came to London in the 1960s. My dad came from the south of Spain, from a city named Jaén, and my mother was from Sevilla. I got to understand in my early years what it meant to be an immigrant. I can only imagine how difficult it was for them to go to a different country, not speaking the language, not having friends or family. Missing the food, the weather. I am so aware of what current generations of immigrants have to go through!

When I was nine, my parents decided they wanted us to have a Spanish upbringing, so we left London and moved back to Spain, settling in Marbella, Malaga.

I had a normal childhood and education. Because my mother tongue was English, I went down a class when I got to Spain, but I recovered and did okay. As I mentioned in the introduction, my father passed away when I was 15; he was 54. It was a shock to me and knocked the whole family in ways I didn't expect.

It was only years later that I realised the impact it had on me and my brother. The usual questions people ask themselves at times of crisis came to me. How could this have happened? How could my dad, the powerful centre of my life, be gone? How could he have died just like that? Was there something I could have done differently? Why had this happened to me while all my friends at school still had their fathers? Why had it happened now? Why, why. . .

Into that whirl of pain, my grandfather bravely stepped in to try to make sure that the family was supported while we overcame the loss. But then we were thrown back into more grief when, six months later, my grandad joined my dad and we were left alone.

I remember looking to my uncles on my father's side for more support. But they did not step up to help and in fact were nowhere to be seen. In six months, two of the main rocks of my life were gone. My mum, my seven-year-old brother and I were alone.

Mum did what so many mums do in times of crisis. She bent herself to the task, working harder and harder to ensure that we were provided for, had food on the table and heat in the house. She was and luckily still is extraordinary, in my eyes and with tears in my eyes I tell you now, she is a legend!

For my part, I carried on studying until I left school at 18. My teen years were marked by a pattern of school, part-time jobs and partying. I worked as a DJ for many years, so access to sex, drugs and rock and roll was very easy, but I always had that sense of responsibility.

The way things were at home, with my mother working all hours possible to pay the debts that had piled up before and after Dad's death, meant that for me going to university wasn't an option and I had to look around to find what else I could do.

With few choices, I joined the army and served 13 months in the military police, where I learned discipline, chain of command, respect, friendship and loyalty. It was a fascinating and empowering time that gave me so many skills in life that I never otherwise would have had. Perhaps strong guidance from senior officers was what I needed now that my dad wasn't around.

I left the army at 19 and needed something to do that would support my mother and family. It was then that I got into sales. This was the period in the 1980s of the great timeshare boom in Spain. I was a kid who spoke English and Spanish. I was as green as anything, but determined to make a go of it as a real estate agent. I remember turning up on my first day at work, being shown the ropes and told 'get selling or you'll be fired'. No pressure then! It involved approaching holidaymakers on the streets and signing them up. I had to learn how to be unafraid, to be likeable and to keep a positive mindset when I got knocked back. And let's face it, in those early days, that was often!

But I stuck with it. I began to understand the way the office was run and I got to know the people who were the developers and landowners we worked for. I watched and learned, and began to think that maybe it wasn't so difficult to do. Call me naive, call me determined, but a year later I started my own real estate business with a partner. I was excited. I was taking my future and my life into my own hands—that sense of being my own boss has always been the place in my mind where I'm the happiest. I was in charge. Or thought I was. I'd gone into partnership with an older man, who, I didn't realise, was a complete psychopath. He was aggressive, dangerous to be around and had no concern for me at all. In fact, I'm convinced at some points he wanted to kill me.

Nevertheless, I learned and I learned more. I found out about people, about how you approach someone to sell them something. I learned which ones would not give you even two seconds of your time. I learned about being friendly and—dare I say it?—charming. And I had success.

Life went along pretty comfortably. I got married to the wonderful Julia, and we had Max. We were living in a nice part of Spain with lots of sunshine. Life was an adventure.

Then, two years in to living the dream, came the first real estate market crash. I had credit cards and bills to pay and suddenly I was down to my last few coins. We were about to lose the house, people were knocking on our door looking for money. I can remember hearing Max crying in the other room because he was hungry. I had kept some savings—just a few coins,—in an old box of Roses chocolates. I went over to it to get money for some food and found all I had left was one 100-pesetas coin. That was it. That was all the money I had in the world. I'd lost everything. Or so I thought at that moment. But I still had a loving family and a wife and child to look after. Plus my wife was pregnant with our second child. I tilted the box to get the coin out and, at that moment, it's also true to say that the penny dropped. I had to act, and act now.

With no other money, the first thing I had to do was make sure my family ate. Believe it or not, I got my son a tin of lentils and after I had bought that I had no more money in the world. The next day I asked a friend if he could give me some work. He agreed and I started inviting people to time-share resorts. . .

And it worked. One week later I was making over $3000–$4000 a month. I was back on track.

So they say that after every dark night there is a brighter day.

I built on what I had. By the age of 27, I was running large sales teams, getting into marketing, running resorts and converting hotels into timeshare resorts.

At the age of 30 I was offered a job working in another property business. I turned it down because it wasn't something I really wanted to do. Then they upped the offer. And upped it again. I was finally offered a ridiculous salary for a job I didn't initially want. Eventually—and this was over 20 years ago—I was offered €6,000 ($7,000 US) a month. I weighed up the offer and decided that it was good, so I took it, with no doubts.

I was on track. I was making hay while the sun shone and, more importantly, I was making money. Once again my boss was a lot older than me, and it is only in hindsight that I realise I was unconsciously looking for a father figure, hoping that someone would fill in the very big gap in my life left by my dad. It was only when my own sons reached the age I was or my brother was when we lost our father that I really began to realise the impact his death had on me. What was I supposed to do as a dad? I had no role model to base my behaviour on. But back then was a different time and a different culture. There were no therapists or psychologists to help, no counselling, either—and men in Spain didn't exactly open up to other men about their feelings. So I got on with trying to do the right thing.

What that experience taught me was a stoical sense of determination. And that realisation came into greater clarity when I created my mantra—something that I think when I'm pushing on and fighting and doing my best: *no one is coming to my rescue*. The fact is, although you may have friends and support around you, understanding quickly that you have to face your challenges head on is the best thing you can do.

Motivational speaker Brendon Burchard phrases it this way: 'Challenge is the pathway to engagement and progress in our lives. But not all challenges are created equal. Some challenges make us feel alive, engaged, connected and fulfilled. Others simply overwhelm us. Knowing the difference as you set bigger and bolder challenges for yourself is critical to your sanity, success and satisfaction.'

Whatever happens, I always remember that it's up to me to take the necessary action. Many spend their lives expecting the perfect solution to be presented to them—whether that's the perfect idea, the perfect job, or just more money to fall in their laps. So many believe someone will come along and want to help you and it will all be perfect. But optimism and naivety are close friends, and unfortunately life and nature have a way of putting egg on faces. When that happens, you have to get up, keep on, don't accept *no*, stop crying and stop feeling sorry for yourself. Take 'response-ability.' Of course you must be responsible, but you must also make sure your response to whatever life throws at you is always the same: get up and try again.

Almost immediately after beginning my new job, my family came to have a lovely way of life. We lived in a large, comfortable house. I had an idyllic family life, great pay and money in the bank, for once. But, after 18 months I got bored. I wanted a challenge again.

So I sold everything I had to have money in the bank to get into real estate, working for myself, starting all over again. The following year I started developing properties and selling real estate. The upshot was that I was soon making a lot of money. Those were happy times, in my early and mid-thirties I was living the dream! House, family, cars, money, motorbikes.

I had it made, right?

Wrong!

At the age of 38 I hit my second real estate crisis. Why I didn't prepare for it after the first one, I don't know, but there's a lesson in that, too. The truth is, I lost everything. I lost all our money. I lost my properties. I lost the cars and the great house we lived in. I say I hit a property crisis— but it's more like it hit me. And although I say I lost everything, really, that's not true. Julia and the kids stuck with me and that's what really counts.

This time, as a nearly middle-aged person, it was much more difficult. I had become used to the wealth and to a very comfortable way of life. I had a Porsche and I had motorbikes, and a lifestyle that suited me and my family very well indeed. Now I was in debt, struggling with the loss of material things I had taken for granted.

What next?

I am a great believer in serendipity. Things happen for a reason. Simon, a friend of mine, was working for the hypnotist and lifestyle expert Paul McKenna. Though I wasn't really impressed with personal development at the time, I heard a talk by Paul and it got me curious. Soon after I read his book *Change Your Life In Seven Days*. I was impressed. There was something in it, an approach to life that I'd never seen before. I wanted to know more and, thanks to my friend and Paul's generosity I was able to do the training for free. I took action and trained with him in London.

My training with Paul McKenna and Dr Richard Bandler lasted for a few years. During that time I absorbed their messages of self-reliance and taking charge of one's emotional life. I remember being in the seminar room with Richard and Paul and, for the first time in my life, I was aware of my thoughts and how to change them and apply them deliberately. I had a set of skills I'd never had before. That in itself was a revelation to me and the powerful techniques Richard and Paul taught for dealing with challenges led me to become a Practitioner in NLP, then a Master Practitioner and a Trainer.

I lost everything for a reason, I told myself. *For some reason I had to hit rock bottom and then come up again, different, changed and with new knowledge.*

At that time, I needed this new way of thinking so much. I was scared, I was frustrated, and I was angry with myself and with the world over what I'd been through and put my family through in gaining so much and then losing everything. . . twice!

And then Paul announced that he was closing his training courses in London to move to Los Angeles. These were the very courses in which I had experienced first hand the extraordinary effects of personal development training and seen other people's lives transformed by NLP.

It was then I received the offer. I was given the chance to continue promoting for Richard and start a new NLP training company that housed Richard Bandler's London seminars. But should I? Could I? It was a very daunting prospect.

I had been a real estate salesman who had plenty of life skills, plenty of experience. But, though I knew how to sell, I knew nothing about running a personal development training business. On the other hand, I knew passionately that my life had been hugely enriched by my connection with the personal development world.

Now there came to me two useful questions that helped me answer my doubts. They went like this:

> *If not me, then who?*
> *If not now, then when?*

And that was it. I committed! Self-help had real value. I knew that. And it was my conviction that made me commit to whatever lay ahead

So, at 42, I was living on the last bit of money we had and it was that transition into this new venture that allowed me to make a living to start all over again; my life completely changed.

It's funny how things can echo from the past. In fact, I made the same trip that my father had made all those years before when he emigrated from Spain to the UK. This was a new journey and a new experience filled with the pain of parting from my family and home, with the excitement of starting in a whole new world and facing all the challenges and learning I would need to do.

It was tough at first. To get things going, I had to leave my family behind in Spain and organise a new life in the UK, starting from nothing. I was in a country where I had never worked before, with very different food, a completely different lifestyle and, maybe most importantly, with a very different expectation about the weather!

Things weren't easy for me. It's hard leaving your family to look for a new future.

I salute you, fellow immigrants. I had a taste of what it must have been like for my parents. My dad emigrated to London after the Spanish Civil War, not speaking a word of English. I at least had that advantage over him. My mum came to London many years later at the age of 17 and they found each other and made a family and a life. That in itself was an achievement. God knows what so many others have to go through all around the world when they are forced to migrate due to war, or economics. I know my story is nothing in comparison to theirs, but my own insight gives me the empathy I believe is so vital when I see someone who needs help.

Building the business took a huge amount of learning. I made mistakes, sure, but I was helped and supported by people along the way and I came through, creating a unique programme committed to encouraging people to help themselves and to help others. It has been ten years since those early days. I want to thank all of those who have had to endure working with me. They have all contributed to helping me arrive at where I stand today.

In this work and the work I've done before, in over 32 years of business, I have developed more brands and businesses than I care to remember. At the same time, I've been a son, a father, a husband, a brother, a friend. I've met many great people. All of this has moulded me into who I am. The great Frank Sinatra said, '*Don't hide your scars. . . they make who you are.*'

From a business point of view, I am a marketer, a salesperson, a CEO, a boss. I am an author, a speaker, an editor of a magazine, a promoter of many great people, a partner, a producer of TV and other content. All this is true. But what I am above all else is a dreamer. From when I was very little, my mum always called me a dreamer. If that means I am a believer that anything is possible and that I can create new things, then I suppose I am. Maybe it's true what friends have said —that I am a leader, a visionary! These are not words I use easily, it's just who I suppose I am. Part of my vision is that I believe we can make this world a much better place and I don't listen to those who tell me it's not possible! I choose to ignore them.

I come from a place where my life has given me vital lessons. My experience, looking around at the personal development from the inside, has also allowed me to see the flaws and mistakes that so many make and keep making. This is, in many ways, priceless for my business.

As for life generally, there have been quite a few missteps, stumbles and falls, a few scares, some very dark and sad days along the way, some very scary ones; but 53 years in, I've never been hungrier to make an impact. It's still difficult at times. Running a business can be very lonely. I have many days when I speak to people who have no idea of what we do as a company, nor of the amazing changes that I see regularly occurring in people's lives. I meet the cynics and the lost, as well as the optimists and the most amazingly talented people. And to all of them I pass on the message that positive change can and does happen every day in people's lives. Sometimes it's hard. Sometimes I believe I'm swimming against the current, alone. But the amazing people I meet along the way and the transformations I witness have made it all worth it.

It has been said before, but it's worth repeating: Remember to be kind. Everyone you meet is fighting a battle you likely know nothing about.

Chapter 2

GREATNESS, SUCCESS, FULFILMENT AND PASSION

In this part we review. . .

What Makes Greatness?

One of the things I really came to realise during my early years of training in personal development is that great people aren't just great in some inexplicable way. They display an attitude and behaviour that makes greatness happen. In many ways, that is the core message of personal and professional growth - that you can learn those attitudes and behaviour, too. That's why my quest in the second part of my life has been to study, model and learn from the greats.

I'm not the only one to do this, of course. Like many others, I'm learning from others all the time. One big inspiration is Tony Robbins. For many years he has been at the forefront of personal development, he has coached world leaders, he has brought personal development to public consciousness by helping and inspiring millions of people around the world. He has also inspired a generation of new leaders in personal development. He's one of many extraordinary figures who know about success and exhibit successful behaviours every single day.

The second part of this book will look in more depth at the attitudes you find in people who've been successful, and at the other common factors I've identified. It will ask what skills people touched by greatness use to succeed, how they are so relentless in their search for whatever it is they are trying to achieve - and will seek to find out what's missing when you aren't pursuing your dream with every fibre of your being.

That last question isn't meant to sound harsh. It's not about blame, it's about identifying what you need to change to free youurself for success. A lot of people don't really 'think' who they want to be or what they want to do and don't know what a successful attitude to life looks like. Some don't even have the time to consider it. *Paying the bills,* or *getting food on the table,* or *life in general,* gets in the way.

I am a great believer in things happening for a reason—are you? For example, when I was younger I obviously wasn't as prepared as I am now to write this book, because I didn't have the knowledge, skills and experience I have now. So, now is the moment to share it with others and give you not just a new insight into my business success, but also the opportunity to learn useful things from the success of others. Things happen at certain times because they're right at that time. Many successful people firmly believe they're destined for success in some way. That is serendipity.

That said, we really need to examine the word - *success.*

Success - What It Is and What It Is Not

In the self-improvement world, *success* comes up time and time again as the thing people aim towards. I've come to realise over my time in this work that a lot of people have the wrong idea about success. Generally, success means to many people, *I have money, I am wealthy and financially independent.* But does that make you successful? I have met and worked with a lot of people in this industry and they are seen as successful, they are wealthy, they have the theory, yet they are miserable.

A little while ago someone asked me if you need to feel fulfilled to feel you are a success. This kind of question is exactly what I mean. It seems like a perfectly simple question on the surface. . . but then think about it a little more.

The word *fulfilment* implies *completion*. It literally means that you are filled fully with a sense of satisfaction, with a sense of achievement. And of course, if you are filled fully, then you cannot be filled any more. Fulfilment and success are therefore often thought of as end points.

There are ways to spot the cracks in this way of thinking about success. You could ask the question the other way round: 'Do you think you can be successful and feel unfulfilled or dissatisfied?'

Speaking with many people described as successful, the answer is an emphatic 'yes'.

Which leads to another question that sheds light on the first: 'Are successful people *ever* satisfied?' In my experience, the answer to that last question is that many are never satisfied, or fulfilled, and that is what drives them on. Once they achieve a goal, they make a new one. Which would seem to be the opposite of what many people think success must be.

Success, then, isn't an end point, it's a direction of travel. Successful people are most often in a state of continual improvement. Yes, things along the way show them they are doing the right things: winning Olympic gold or making another business deal. . . but that is not success. That is the by-product of the process of successful thinking.

The word *success* is used in many other different ways, yet people don't really think about what they mean by it.

For example, it can be used to mean simple goal-setting. 'I'm going to earn five million dollars next year', or, 'I'm going to finish writing my story by Tuesday'.

If you achieve those goals, then you can say you have been successful at achieving them.

This is a very different definition of *success* from another group of people, who use the word *success* in an unlimited and unfocused way.

For them, success is a vague idea of wellbeing that showers looks, money, houses, cars and benign events on you. It sees the outcome of success-oriented behaviour but doesn't recognise the process that got those outcomes. It makes the idea of success seem like a gift from on high. That isn't success, that is a fairy tale.

Being successful, is not about a single goal or endpoint, nor is it about having some imaginary blessed life.

Being successful is a process of being and becoming.

It also changes its meaning over time in a person's life.

For example, the success of Bill Gates in his 20s at organising the coding for a new operating system and making big bucks out of it is very different from the success he experiences now.

Back in the 1970s, he was driven by excitement at making an operating system that would be used the world over. That drive made him a billionaire. It is fair to say, he was a success!

But that is not what Bill Gates is working toward now. Now, he sees meaning in life in a different way and rather than accumulating *more* wealth, he is actively *disposing* of his wealth. He is doing positive work with the Bill Gates Foundation, looking for solutions to illness, poverty and famine.

Once again, he is in the *process* of doing this work, permanently. It's not that he will stop one day and say: 'There is no more polio in the world, thanks to me.' In fact, he is destined every day to wake up to carry on eradicating illnesses or empowering the poor, or inspiring people to take action, because the bigger problem of inequality of resources, wealth and opportunity will be around for a very long time. So, in a way, every day, he faces failure and continues on with specific goals, knowing there is a bigger problem out there. The fact he thinks in such a way and carries on is an indicator of his successful attitude to life.

As for fulfilment and satisfaction— he may feel fulfilled in his work, or satisfied, but he may not. It's not like he's going to kick back and lounge in the sun all day. That's not what drives him.

Satisfied can be another misleading word, also implying an end point. It comes from 'sated' and once again implies 'full up'. Taking Bill Gates as the example again, his drive means he wants to continue doing great work. He is not 'full up' with helping people. He is not 'fed up' either. His 'failure' and dissatisfaction at his sense of there being a job that is not yet done do not deter him. They are part of his successful thinking.

Then there is that other word: *happiness.*

For many people, happiness is the indicator of success, rather than money or medals. But this, once again, is subjective. After all, being happy is not exclusively an indication that you've been successful. It might also be an indicator of having low standards!

I joke— but do you see how much of a weasel word *success* is when you think about it? It isn't one thing. It's lots of things in different contexts, and some ideas about success are more like religious belief than the nuts and bolts of life.

Find the right words to define where you are. Smell the roses! Enjoy where you are, enjoy what you have achieved. Part of the problem is that we keep seeking to measure success with a goal, such as a bigger car, a bigger house, or more money in the account. And that's not it. Success is the attitude that leads you to improve and change and move on every day, it's a mindset that keeps you engaged with and interested in the world, and that drives your plans to come to fruition.

'Peace is the result of retraining your mind to process life as it is, rather than as you think it should be.'
—Wayne W. Dyer

My Success and Successes

So, am I a success?

I have a business, and I am always pushing onward to make it better. I don't think solely about one end point. It's also the process. Everything you do along the way to make things happen and the passion in your heart so you are fully engaged with all your soul—that is the indication of your success.

So, can I say I have success? In one area, yes, I am proud. My truly greatest success and legacy to the world are my kids: three amazing, outgoing, charismatic, loving, admired, respected and loved kids. Kids who have the right values, with a great work ethic and who are entrepreneurial. They are my success.

Other parents will understand that. I've done the best I could, and I know I could have—should have—done more for them and maybe they've learned as much as they can from me–but if there is anything the old man is still teaching them, it is that I keep going on reinventing, keep evolving, and keep going and going. The *Never Give Up* approach!

From a business point of view, I've had many successes. My current work began, as I mentioned, with NLP. I have contributed to training nearly 30,000 people.

So far, through the first four Best You EXPOs I have promoted, over 25,000 delegates have attended the 500 workshops and seminars. I am also proud of our The Best You objective where we are aiming to reach 150 million people in the next five years.

We have trained or reached tens of thousands of people and I have produced content that has reached millions more. But I don't stop because I've achieved that. I go on. There are always new challenges. That is the nature of life.

I used to be baffled when people announced they were giving up their fortunes. *Why?* I thought. *They took so long to build them up!* But I realise too, that there comes a point in people's lives when success for themselves is no longer enough. People evolve. In the same way in private life people often go on to understand that living a successful life is about taking care of their loved ones - they realise that in growing a business, success comes when they care about customers and employees. Then, there's a stage beyond that, which is to take that responsibility globally. That is when people start to see the good they can do with the money they have.

Maybe you'll be part of that, too.

When you realise you can do things for the world—leave a large legacy for others to help them succeed in their lives—realise that life is bigger than just you and your family—then the idea of taking responsibility extends not just to your family, friends and employees, but out on a global scale.

You will probably understand this easier if you are a parent, but I'm sure it can work for anyone. Ultimate love is complete selflessness, which makes sacrifice something positive. Others' success is your success.

Sure, I want to live the most fulfilled life and make the maximum positive mark I can on this planet—but I would love so much more for my kids and their generation to do so much better, and I believe they will because we have messed up a lot of things for future generations.

Keep in mind the **Dalai Lama's** often-repeated quote: *'When we feel love and **kindness** toward **others**, it not only makes **others** feel loved and cared for, but it **helps** us also to develop inner happiness and peace'.* Or another one of my favourites from an anonymous source: *'Helping one person might not change the world, but it could change the world for one person.'*

The Question to ask yourself:
How much of your time do you spend helping people, and is it enough?
It doesn't take much to change someone's life. Sometimes all it takes is a few kind words or an action. Helping someone. Letting them know you see them, and that you're there to help them.

Passion

All of this sounds great—but I've missed out the most important thing. Passion—having a passion to do the thing you're doing, and doing it well.

To release the energy that brings you success in whatever path you choose, you need to throw yourself into it with **every fibre** of your being, to engage your whole, true self, without holding back. You commit to your path like you commit to your marriage, into loving your kids or loved ones, with every part of yourself. You're not a part-timer—you're into what you want to do, fully, completely, unendingly. The passion is the thing that will drive you on, that will make you realise how you can't stop, but have to continue on. Passion—that's the emotion that drives everything else, so you throw yourself into your work.

To become successful you have to do what you love and do it with passion. Putting that emotion, that drive, that fire to work every day will make new successes.

Passion is the secret ingredient to successful thinking. It's the fuel and it's the food on which successful behaviour feeds.

A quote I have used nearly all my life is '*All or Nothing*'. When it comes to passion, it has to be ALL IN, all the time!

In Chapter 6 I will talk about purpose. Someone asked me recently how I find my purpose. The answer is by constantly asking myself questions. It's vital that you make time to think critically about your life, so that it doesn't pass you by.

The questions to ask yourself:

What are you really passionate about?

What gets you super excited?

What do you LOVE doing?

If you didn't have to work to earn money, what would you do with your time?

I believe you find purpose when you start living a passionate life and do things with passion. Which also works the other way round: when you find what you are passionate about, you will find your purpose.

Chapter 3

INNER YOU— THE THREE KEY TRAITS OF SUCCESSFUL PEOPLE

Over my years of working with the greats in the self-improvement world, I've seen some extraordinary changes in people they've helped, and observed up close the skills these gurus use.

I've seen people who were flattened and completely demoralised pick themselves up and go after their goals. I've seen people at absolute rock bottom with nothing other than the clothes on their backs find a way up, learn self-reliance and become self-motivated and engaged with life again. I've seen people helped to overcome their fears, those who were struggling given a new attitude to life, and those unsure of how to achieve their aims reach them. In the world of NLP, where I first began my own journey, the emphasis is not only on getting what you want in life, but also on teaching you to think and to help others do the same. This is one of the most important things in the world of personal development that is not spoken about enough—the ability to pay it forward.

I will write later about nurturing an attitude of gratitude, which is linked to the ability to help others get on in life. It is an extraordinary truth that many people who show genuine gratitude for the blessings the world has bestowed on them discover that the world finds ways to help them more. Some people say this is because the planet is 'resonating at the same frequency' as the grateful person, and so gratitude breeds more gratitude. Others simply say that by opening yourself to an optimistic view of the world in which you realistically recognise those opportunities where you can help others and others help you, you notice more of that side of reality. Our minds, after all, are filters—and if we are expecting conflict in the world, we are much more likely to find it. However, having gratitude isn't the same thing as naively hoping the world will do you good, and not recognising the existence of the mean, manipulative people in it.

It is a question of where you decide to put your focus.

Recognising the good in the world seems to draw it to you.

This is the way many successful people organise their worlds. They genuinely believe that the universe will provide them with what they want. Some people have it late in life, but they have that 'aha' moment, when suddenly everything makes sense.

This also comes from flexibility in thinking, from opening yourself to opportunities. How often have you heard people say, when talking about their success, 'I didn't plan this to happen. I was working toward something different, but then this opportunity presented itself'? Recognition of opportunity comes from following a feeling that the universe is on your side.

This way of thinking is the foundation of international book and film phenomenon *The Secret*, and it's what lies behind ideas such as *The Law of Attraction*. Is it a law? No, not in a strict *scientific* sense. But it is a way of organising the mind. It is a way of having faith, and keeping faith during the tough times.

With faith, a belief that the universe is on your side, come other skills that I'm going to look at in the coming chapters. Life isn't only about seizing opportunities—it's about pushing on when things aren't necessarily easiest. It's about reaching the point at which the universe does indeed provide. While you are getting there, there are plenty of things you need to do to stay on course. Cultivating an attitude of curiosity and openness to the world, to change, to adapt, is only part of the story.

Being ready to push on and go for what you want is absolutely central to becoming 'The Best You'. In *The Secret*, author **Rhonda Byrne** advises you to look for the positives and what is useful to you—and to *keep looking*. Some people get disheartened and give up if they don't get what they want immediately. What is vital, especially during the difficult times, is that that you don't give up. Keep on toward your goal.

This attitude should be the foundation of who you are and who you will become.

There three great skills are central to the journey of so many people who've enjoyed success. I call them *The New Three Rs*.

When people used to talk about education in the old days, the *Three Rs* used to be *reading, writing and arithmetic*. In the realm of education for personal development, which is a whole different form of education, the *New Three Rs* means something different. They are:

- Resilience

- Revolution

- Reinvention.

With these three skills you will be able to keep yourself going throughout your life. Cultivate them. At different times, you will rely on each. Sometimes you will need to be undeterred and focused, despite setbacks. At others, you will need to turn over old ways of thinking and come up with whole new attitudes. At others again, you will need to learn from events to create new ways of thinking about yourself and the work you do.

Like a cat, you will land on your feet.

Unlike a cat, you will have more than nine lives.

Resilience, Revolution and Reinvention are central skills to getting what you want. I'm now going to look at each in more detail.

Resilience

One dictionary definition of resilience is: 'The ability to bounce or spring back into shape after being stretched, bent or compressed'.

There's an old story of the Scottish rebel Robert the Bruce, who was in hiding from the English in a cave, where he took refuge and lived for three months. He had reached the lowest point of his life. His armies were defeated, he was on the run and the English were after him. Robert was alone when he saw a spider attempting to weave a web. Robert became increasingly intrigued by the spider that was climbing up one side of an opening to the cave and kept launching itself across the space, only to get blown back again. It struggled on for what seemed like hours, repeatedly knocked back down again. And finally, just when Robert was giving up on believing the spider could succeed, it did it. It leapt across the gap and began to weave a web.

Robert the Bruce was so strengthened by the sight of the spider's eventual success that he vowed he would not give up his fight. A few years later, Robert the Bruce led his men against the English at Bannockburn, defeating them despite the Scots being outnumbered ten to one.

The moral of the story is often stated: 'If at first you don't succeed, try, try again.'

Whatever the truth of the tale, we've all seen or met those people who never accept defeat. They get knocked down, then 'pick themselves up, dust themselves off, and start all over again', as the old song goes.

Resilience is actually a mixture of skills.

In part, it's about being able to reframe failure as a learning experience. It's about ignoring frustration (which can so often lead to a sense of helplessness), and also changing despondency to something else—sometimes anger, but more usefully, determination.

Resilience is one of the skills mastered by people who handle stress well. They are able to get through difficult moments by making their emotions more manageable, by shrinking down the problems they face, or learning a mindfulness that enables them to transcend what they are going through.

The mixture of skills needed for resilience even seems to incorporate opposites. Keeping focused on the goal is one part of resilience, while being flexible is also vital. That means being willing to try new things to move on, not engaging in negative emotions, but keeping the positives in sight.

Whichever type of resilience works for them, resilient people bounce back from setbacks and are grateful for life's simple pleasures, seeing them as evidence of eventual success.

Resilient people often reframe setbacks through their faith, telling themselves 'everything happens for a reason'. For them, whatever event occurs, it's a learning experience provided by the universe. That is a deeply empowering attitude.

Some people are resilient from an early age. Maybe it's true to say they are 'born resilient'. Nothing seems to bother them or deter them, and they have a natural way of getting the best from themselves.

But have no doubt, resilience is not just an innate trait, just as many other behaviours aren't innate. It is a skill which some people adopt and learn from very early on. It's a skill anybody can learn.

I believe resilience is the foundation for all other life events. It's the iron and concrete you are made of. In my years of watching people succeed, I have not come across any successful person or game changer who doesn't have it. Of course, there are those who were born into privilege and thus do not appear to experience setbacks—but then, those people are often taught resilience by their parents or at their school. It's part of their early training for success.

Those who don't master how to be resilient struggle. And that's why, just like the privileged people who were taught it, it's vital to learn how to do it.

Many of us don't find out how resilient we are until we face a test or problem. We all have it within us, provided the goal means enough to us. I've never come across any successful person who hasn't struggled and had to draw on their resilience.

If you are a parent, you know that you would do anything to keep your child safe. You wouldn't be deterred or knocked down, but would get up again and again if your loved one were faced with immediate danger. The fact is, when push comes to shove you *will* do what it takes if the stakes are high enough.

And the best bit is that resilience can be learned, so you can use it when you need it. You just need to tap into it. Further on I will show you how you can develop your resilience.

Studies in Resilience

The world is full of amazing and resilient people. It's worth learning from their stories.

What are the factors of resilience? **Nelson Mandela**, who was imprisoned for 27 years on Robben Island as a political prisoner, never gave up his belief that he would eventually succeed in his goals. This is because he had a sense of Personal Mission. Indeed, many resilient people have strong faith and a belief that everything happens for a reason.

Thanks to his resilience, Mandela was able to maintain his concentration and focus on his core objective, and at the same time manage his emotions. It must have been incredibly difficult, yet through all that time he kept his emotions from destroying him.

Remember, too, my comment that not making it all about you is central to being a better person? Mandela was part of a larger movement. He was doing good for the oppressed people of South Africa. His ordeal wasn't just about him. Mandela knew where he was heading and never stopped believing.

It's said that **Thomas Edison** failed 1000 times before creating the lightbulb. This is one of those convenient numbers that you often hear in the personal development world, but there's no doubt that his 'failures' were numerous. Some people say his attempts numbered between 1000 and 10,000 but, whatever the reality, it's agreed that Edison failed a lot of times before he successfully created a reliable, working lightbulb. His response to his repeated failures was to reframe them, famously saying: 'I have not failed. I've just found 10,000 ways that won't work.'

Oprah Winfrey had a harrowing childhood, in which she was repeatedly raped by family members. She ran away from home and gave birth when she was just 14, and lost her child soon after. Her estranged father then took charge of her life, encouraging her to put her past behind her and focus on what she wanted to achieve. Oprah responded to the tough father figure, who gave her days shape and a goal to aim for. Her focus on getting what she wanted and getting away from her past led her to excel as an honours student in high school. She went on to win an oratory contest, and secured a full scholarship at university. Oprah is now a global brand admired by hundreds of millions, and worth around $3 billion.

Stephen King had his first novel rejected 30 times. If it weren't for Tabitha, King's wife, *Carrie* may never have been published. After so much constant rejection, King threw his manuscript in the rubbish bin. Tabitha, retrieved it and made him persevere. Stephen's books have sold over 350 million copies and have been made into countless major motion pictures.

Similarly, **Agatha Christie** suffered five years of continual rejection before getting her first book deal. To date, sales of her books have been in excess of $2 billion. **J K Rowling**, famously a single mum living in Edinburgh after a failed marriage, was rejected 12 times. When Bloomsbury agreed to go ahead, her editor told her there was no money in writing children's books. The last four novels of the Harry Potter series each consecutively became the fastest-selling books in history, on both sides of the Atlantic, with combined sales in excess of 450 million. **Jack Canfield and**

Mark Victor Hansen received 140 rejections before the *Chicken Soup for the Soul* series sold 125 million copies.

The Beatles were told that guitar groups were on the way out and they had no future in show business. **Steven Spielberg** was rejected by the University of Southern California before he was accepted. He then dropped out of university and went on to become one of the world's most successful movie directors.

In all these stories, focus and self belief were absolutely central, plus in Stephen King's case, a little bit of support at the right time.

For those who think that failure is not part of the narrative for successful people, Michael Jordan has some great advice: 'I have missed more than 9000 shots in my career. I have lost almost 300 games. On 26 occasions I have been entrusted to take the game-winning shot, and I missed. I have failed over and over and over again in my life. And that is why I succeed.'

It pays to continue on, learn from mistakes and keep pursuing your goals.

What Resilience Is Not

Everyone has problems in their lives, challenges from the big to the small. It's what you choose to do with those challenges that is key to whether or not you have yet learned the art of resilience.

I've seen a lot of people over the years who really don't know how lucky they are. Their lack of skills at handling stress only make their own lives more miserable. There's an event which may potentially inconvenience you, and there's your stressed reaction to the event. A lot of people really don't see the difference between the two.

It means they handle straightforward situations with extreme emotions. By cussing, complaining and bitching they generally make their own lives miserable, when the situation they're in doesn't deserve the rage or despair they're throwing at it. A more clear-thinking person would just shrug and get on with it. That shrug is resilience.

Let's face it, for a lucky family, a stressful day might be getting stuck in traffic and getting to the place they planned to spend the day two hours later than they expected. For some people, deep stress might come from having a six-hour delay at the airport. For others it might be sacrificing a holiday abroad for a local one. Yet none of these things in themselves are disasters. They don't have to be made into one.

I've seen some people lose their cool because the boiler isn't working and they don't have hot water for a day. They spend their day raging and fuming, where others might stay solution-focused or seek alternatives. Some might even get triggered because they have to wait two or three minutes for their shower water to come out warm.

These are tiny problems. Yet, each and every day, people make their own lives miserable by overreacting to these and countless other irritations that in the grand scheme of things make little difference to anyone's life.

The Question: How do you respond to the things that irritate you? What about mildly bad news? Do you just react, or do you respond more consciously?

Resilience—or its absence—is found in such simple everyday events. If you make a big deal out of something that in reality is easily managed, then the thing that needs to be changed is not out there in the world, it is in you. Don't like the sound of that? Then how do you expect your life to be? Are you going to try to force other people and events to do exactly what you want all the time? That will make you and everyone around you extremely unhappy.

I sometimes say to people who are heading down the dark tunnel of complaining about the tiniest things, or who are not taking responsibility for their lives. . . *So what! Who cares? Get real!*

In my talks and seminars I often ask the question—*who here complains?*

Usually, it's just a handful of people who'll admit to it, but we know it's not true. And you? Be honest (and we will discuss honesty later in the book)—do you complain when you could be doing something more useful? Think about it—how many times a day and about what?

The truth is whatever you do, wherever you are, whatever you have, or whatever may be your case, there are many, many people all around the world who are responding to much more difficult situations than you and in a much smarter way.

They know that the energy of complaint creates a victim mentality. That is not a useful habit of mind.

Sometimes comparison is a useful way to get your own sense of distance and perspective on problems. If you think about your problems, and more importantly how you are responding to them, then consider the lot of people who are fleeing for their lives with their family and kids from a country at war. Suddenly your life challenges might seem a little petty. How would you respond in that situation? Would you carry on complaining, knowing that many of your loved ones have died, knowing you have nothing, that you don't know where your next meal will come from and that, unless you do something, death will follow? Is complaining going to help you? Or will you need to start to deal with things, take responsibility for what you can do and push on? Your choice. In such comparisons you see the real roots of resilience and perhaps begin to see that you need a new way to respond to the world rather than complaining—and that many other people already have this. It's time for you to learn how to do that, too.

Resilience is a trait I admire so much in people. To be able to survive with very little and still share what you have and smile is a remarkable feat. True resilience is not only to survive, but to keep your mind open to new chances and opportunities, even when it all seems hopeless.

So, resilience isn't necessarily about being tough. It's about being true to yourself and not getting lost or disheartened at the first setback, putting things in perspective, remaining cool when others panic. There are many ways to do it— but the more subtle side of resilience, I think, is summed up in a quote I love:

> '*You must be shapeless, formless, like water. When you pour water in a cup, it becomes the cup. When you pour*

water in a bottle, it becomes the bottle. When you pour water in a teapot, it becomes the teapot. Water can drip and it can crash. Become like water my friend.'

—Bruce Lee

Rudyard Kipling's much-quoted poem *If* also speaks to that other important aspect of resilience: the ability to keep true to yourself.

*If you can keep your head when all about you
Are losing theirs and blaming it on you,
If you can trust yourself when all men doubt you,
But make allowance for their doubting too;
If you can wait and not be tired by waiting,
Or being lied about, don't deal in lies,
Or being hated, don't give way to hating,
And yet don't look too good, nor talk too wise:*

*If you can dream—and not make dreams your master;
If you can think—and not make thoughts your aim;
If you can meet with Triumph and Disaster
And treat those two impostors just the same;
If you can bear to hear the truth you've spoken
Twisted by knaves to make a trap for fools,
Or watch the things you gave your life to, broken,
And stoop and build 'em up with worn-out tools:*

*If you can make one heap of all your winnings
And risk it on one turn of pitch-and-toss,
And lose, and start again at your beginnings
And never breathe a word about your loss;
If you can force your heart and nerve and sinew
To serve your turn long after they are gone,*

And so hold on when there is nothing in you
Except the Will which says to them: 'Hold on!'

If you can talk with crowds and keep your virtue,
Or walk with Kings—nor lose the common touch,
If neither foes nor loving friends can hurt you,
If all men count with you, but none too much;
If you can fill the unforgiving minute
With sixty seconds' worth of distance run,
Yours is the Earth and everything that's in it,
And—which is more—you'll be a man, my son!

Of course, let me be clear, the amazing sentiment in that poem appeals to sons and daughters—men and women—equally. It's a powerful poem everyone can learn from.

The truth is, some people appear to be born resilient—nothing seems to bother them. They grow up to become adventurers and strivers in whatever walk of life, from astronauts, through athletes and politicians to shrewd business people who never get knocked down. However, resilience is not a substance or a simple trait—it is a series of skills that can be learned by anybody. And it is something we must all endeavour to gain.

* * *

The Questions you need to ask yourself:

If you had nothing but needed your family to survive, what would you be willing to do?

If you had to learn something in order to restart your life, what would that be?

How many hours would you be willing to work or how many jobs would you be willing to do to meet your commitments?

If your mental health or your life depended on your physical health, how many hours would you spend in the gym?

If the only option you had was to study something to create a new career, what would that be?

The seven key traits that will make you resilient

1. Practise getting your reactions under control. Stress responses can be lessened by exercise and meditation. An excellent tool to de-stress is yoga, but there are many other forms of relaxation you can try. Just make sure you have a regular regime—mornings can be great for de-stressing and will set you up for the day. Not only will you get rid of previous stress, but you will be better able to handle future stress.

2. Flexibility means you won't break under pressure. There is a fable about the mighty oak tree and the blade of grass, which tells the story of why you should be flexible in your emotional and thought responses to difficult situations. The proud oak tree every day reminds the blade of grass how strong he is, how tall and unyielding. The blade of grass agrees and carries on growing. Then, one day, a hurricane blows across the field where they grow. The oak tree digs in its roots and resists the wind, laughing at the blade of grass who has blown flat. But the wind grows stronger and eventually uproots the oak. When the wind dies down, the tree has been blown over, but the blade of grass has sprung back up.

You can learn more about flexibility when you learn how to get in charge of your emotions and your responses. Training can show you how to do that.

3. Look for those you trust. Often a stressful situation happens when you are let down by a colleague. Don't rely on those you can't trust—and always be aware that even those you do might let you down. Take a mentor— someone who is outside of the immediate fray who can offer impartial advice. Do the same with friends and colleagues. Seek opinions and chart your course accordingly with the voices you trust in your ears.

4. Reframe. When a storm cloud appears, look for the silver lining. You can find a way to turn a bad situation around and use it to your advantage.

   Listen to your internal dialogue, listen to yourself and hear how ridiculous you sound sometimes when you are freaking out for the most ridiculous situations.

   This is absolutely at the heart of resilience—to realise that there are countless opportunities available to you, whatever situation you are in.

5. Be grateful. You may not see great reasons to be grateful to the world when the chips are down—but actually this mindset enables you to move on, with lessons learned. Gratitude is a fascinating and powerful trait that once again puts you in charge of difficult situations. Besides, how does moaning help you move forward? Compare the outcomes of maintaining a negative mindset and a positive one. With the positive one, you will grasp those

opportunities. With the negative one, you will miss them because you are too busy playing the victim.

6. A spiritual sense can be a powerful guide. Many entrepreneurs develop a sense of destiny—an unshakeable faith in a higher power that has their wellbeing in mind. It's sometimes harder as you get older to embrace such an idea—but those who succeed often report feeling that the universe is on their side. Getting in tune with and admiring your world is the way to go.

7. Do something. It's all too easy to be frozen by inaction after a shock. Sometimes it is necessary to take stock of where you are to ensure you aren't simply reacting. But being ready to move on, to act on new plans and recoup what you need to is part of recovering.

Relax, meditate and look for what the feedback from the stressful incident has given you. Learn from your mistakes, and then move on. Stress is a tool to strengthen your responses. Coping with it and learning from it will make you resilient, and more able to do things better in future.

Revolution

You can't be who you want to become by being who you are today. Since the beginning of time, revolutions have been necessary for society to evolve. My invitation to you is to start looking at change as your new best friend.

Napoleon Hill said, '*Every adversity, every failure, every heartache carries with it the seed of an equal or greater benefit*'.

The word 'revolution' comes from the Latin *revolutio*. At first meaning 'to roll back or unwind', it also came to mean 'to turn over'—and from there it was a quick step to meaning the overthrow of the established order. A revolution is a change that occurs rapidly and massively, leading to a fundamental transformation.

In the past, we've seen Agricultural, Industrial, and Information Revolutions. I believe we are now in a period of Educational Revolution. Let's just take a quick look and see what each revolution meant at the time for those who lived through them.

The Agricultural Revolution

Let's look at the situation in Britain before the Agricultural Revolution. In the 16th century, farming was still being done along the same feudal lines as it had been done for hundreds of years since the Normans invaded.

Society was heavily dominated by the aristocracy, with local squires and lords controlling the land. Most people lived without the basic things we take for granted in the modern age—running water, a reliable heat source, sanitation—even money. To pay their rent, many people paid in produce. When a crop failed due to a bad season or blight, people starved. Life was precarious, tough and joyless. That was the downside of the pastoral idyll.

There were problems with agriculture. Farmers owned, through marriage and inheritance, strips of land dotted around the strip farming system. Strips were separated from neighbours' by areas of raised earth called baulks, that no-one could plant. If the neighbour's strip was badly tended, weeds and blight spread quickly to your crop. Labour was intensive and back-breaking from morning till night, and at harvest the Church took a tenth of your produce. Few saw any money, but traded in goods in a subsistence lifestyle.

Poverty was king, and families were at the mercy of weather and disease. Research suggests that famine was known by most generations throughout the Middle Ages in Britain, affecting lifespan, killing many young children and leading to starvation in many communities. This was your life.

The land you worked probably didn't belong to you anyway, or there was no proof of it, and you might be there by custom or with no legal proof of tenure. If you were a freeholder or a copyholder with the right documentation, you could prove your claim. If not, you lived a precarious, insecure existence.

Near your village there was the Common Land. Owned collectively by the community, it was never improved or worked effectively, and was used to graze cattle.

In this Feudal System, everything depended on the local squire being responsible and running things fairly.

This way of life was turned upside down by the Agricultural Revolution. It was not one thing, not one change, but a connected series of increasingly accelerating changes that completely reshaped society.

Changes come one by one. With no fertiliser for the fields, the soil in the old system degraded as crops grew. Improvements during the Agricultural Revolution included the four-field crop rotation system, which meant you grew different crops in your field each year so as not to draw all the goodness from the soil. Every fourth year, you left a field to lie fallow, and hopefully recover, before resuming planting. With this system, at any one time, you were only able to produce food on three-quarters of your land.

Farming pioneer Arthur Young wrote of his travels in France, telling how French winemakers improved soil with manure and brought the process of marling the soil to Britain. Jethro Tull invented the seed drill, which planted seeds efficiently in rows rather than scattering them so that many were lost. Numerous other innovations occurred.

These changes relied on one big change, which meant a land grab by the moneyed classes. In many parts of Britain, landowners realised that improvements in wool prices meant they would make more money with fewer people on the land and more sheep.

They swept away the feudal past and created a wealthier, more productive agricultural sector. It had a terrible downside.

The change dispossessed anyone who couldn't prove land ownership. The turmoil led to hundreds of thousands being made homeless and the creation of a massive unemployed class desperate for work.

In Scotland, the Agricultural Revolution saw firstly the Lowland Clearances, and later, the Highland Clearances. In the latter, Clan members were thrown off ancestral lands. One account from the Outer Hebrides tells how 'the richest commoner' in Scotland, Colonel John Gordon of Cluny, ordered the people who lived on his island of South Uist to attend a compulsory meeting. Once there, they were forced aboard waiting ships and transported to the USA and Canada against their will.

Those who ran away were hunted down with dogs. Many arrived on the shores of Nova Scotia with only the clothes they stood up in. Transplanted to a foreign land, where the winters were much crueller, many of those thousands of enforced emigrants died. This was late in the history of the British Agricultural Revolution, which started in England in the 1560s. The clearance of South Uist happened in 1851.

It is one of the most extreme stories of the abuse of power that happened during the Agricultural Revolution. But across Britain, farm labourers and former small farmers were thrown off their land. It really was a revolution. It overthrew the established order and brought massive change, suffering and even death for many in the short term. The longer effect was to make people wealthier by making food more easily available and by ending the cycle of famine in Britain.

The Industrial Revolution

The Industrial Revolution was in many ways a continuation of the Agricultural Revolution. The questing mind of inventors and reformers applied scientific thinking to old methods of production. The village blacksmith who worked iron created from small-scale ore extraction and smelting was eventually replaced by massive industrial foundries. New methods of mechanised cloth production saw small weavers and spinners who produced hand-made cloth in cottage industries replaced with huge mills that used mechanisation to make production more efficient.

The British Empire at first set up trading posts in India, then subjugated the subcontinent. At the time India was one of the wealthiest countries in the world. Britain stripped India of its wealth and made it dependent on British trade. Indian cotton was imported to Britain where value was added by turning it into textiles, and then exported back to India. Empire was a ruthless business. Literally.

In Britain, to support the vast leap in trade, canals were built to transport newly made goods from sites that were never previously accessible to development. Steam power changed the game again, first with Newcomen's atmospheric engine, and later with Watt's double condenser. Richard Trevithick invented an early steam locomotive and George Stephenson improved on it. The pace of change accelerated further. The great industrial mills were no longer dependent on water to transport their goods, and communication improved. The first transatlantic telegraph cable between Britain and the USA was laid in 1858. The world was opening in a way none had imagined.

The Industrial Revolution changed completely the way people lived. Not always for the better. For those swept up helplessly in its progress who hadn't been able to get ahead of the tide of history, life was terrible. Work in coal mines and cotton factories led to horrendous injuries, death and diseases. Children lost limbs in the mines, developed respiratory diseases in the cotton mills, or were killed by the mill machinery.

There were those who resisted change. Ned Ludd was an apprentice weaver working in Britain in the 18th century just as the Industrial Revolution began. He saw the new weaving machines as a threat to his livelihood and broke some of them, supposedly in a fit of rage. Later, his actions inspired a movement of machine breakers who raided factories and destroyed the new equipment in the North of England. The machine breakers became known as Luddites. Of course, the Luddites didn't win. The Industrial Revolution went on without them.

Change will happen no matter what. It is our job to adjust to what is happening and find the opportunities that will help us prosper. If you close yourself off from change, you are going to lose.

There is no doubt that, for many years, working people struggled and suffered thanks to the Industrial Revolution. There's also no doubt that the nation's lives and health improved as society began to catch up with the changes the Industrial Revolution brought. Today, our lives are a world away from the impoverished lives led before the Agricultural and Industrial Revolutions.

But that is not the end of the story. More change came and so much more is in motion now.

The Information Revolution

The clean energy that came with the mass generation of electricity and supply of gas changed people's lives for the better. Electricity became the safe, clean source of power for the modern world. The electric light, the radio, the tram, the train, electrically powered factories heralded the change to a reliance on electricity.

Then the world changed again as electricity was put to a new use.

The foundations of computing were laid down by Charles Babbage in the 19th century, in which he imagined the core elements of a programmable computer, and even included punch cards in the process. Babbage's computer was based on the physical technology of the time, not electronics, which were yet to be invented. Nevertheless, his brilliantly envisioned principles for the Analytical Engine underpinned the great inventions of the early computers.

The technology finally caught up with Babbage's vision in the 1940s in the UK, with the creation of Colossus—the first digital programmable computer—used by the British Secret Services for codebreaking. ENIAC, a faster and more flexible computer, was built by the Americans in 1946.

The Information Revolution had begun, which to this day has seen an increasing acceleration of the capabilities of computers.

From massive machines built in the 1950s and 1960s, the computer has reduced so far that you can hold huge computing power in the palm of your hand. The pace of change has been extraordinary. It is often said that the computing power in a modern smartphone far exceeds the computing power used for the Apollo moon landings.

The changes to people's lives have been equally huge, in ways that were never foreseen in the early days of computing. It is difficult to take in the impact of computing on society.

At one level, computing made many more menial roles easier and eventually unnecessary. Computers control manufacturing processes. Take, for example, car production, which is largely done by robots, with far fewer people on production lines. Car engines are controlled and optimised by computers, which also control on-board entertainment, communication, GPS, air-conditioning, security, emissions and lighting. Orders for cars are taken over the internet, allowing bespoke vehicle manufacture on the production line. The car company's payroll is managed by a small team on computers, where 50 years ago there would have been numerous people in the accounts department.

The insurance taken out by drivers on cars is calculated by computers, the accounts through which the insurance money is paid are computerised, the driver's licence and details are on a government database, making it possible to check for fraudulent claims automatically. . . and so on. In every aspect of people's lives, computers and information make people's lives easier, or—if you haven't caught up with computer technology—make you bang your head against a wall!

But the real power in the Information Revolution is not in the individual transactions computers help with, but in the data attached to them. Private companies and businesses know about your family, your friends, your secret affairs, your bank balance, your spending patterns, your mental health, your fitness, your habits, your politics, your religion. Private companies and governments probably know more about you than your family and closest friends. They listen and log your speech patterns to make your life easier.

All of these things, just as in previous revolutions, have their upsides and their downsides. There is a genuine problem with the end of net neutrality, in which higher paying customers are preferred by internet servers over those with a lower budget. Already, computers analyse which customers seeking customer support have a larger income. Those who are wealthier are routed through to a human being, while those who are not considered good customers are left to struggle with slower and more laborious automated systems. It means that the wealthy can enjoy an entirely different experience of life in society, with no idea what others are going through, separated by monetary value into those who will have a positive experience and those who will fight with poor service.

This seems to be a minor issue, but if it is replicated throughout society, then social mobility becomes more difficult and democracy suffers, as classes become entrenched by the biases inherent in computer programming. The poor are held back and the wealthy preferred. And neither realises their experience of life is not a 'standard' experience.

In warfare, fully autonomous military drones are a step away. How will those drones be programmed? How will they make decisions about who lives and dies? Vehicles will need to make decisions about which way to swerve in a collision that will lead to the least harm. These are genuine ethical problems, not just matters of good programming.

The problems of surveillance and what will happen with the information collected from it has yet to be addressed properly and will raise more issues in the coming years. So will the increasing levels of automation that will make 'filler' jobs obsolete. Human-operated taxis and grocery delivery will disappear. Shopkeepers will be able to replace staff (indeed, they already are, with self-checkout systems). As artificial intelligence grows, it isn't just the menial jobs that are going. As algorithms are developed to mimic the best in human judgement, white collar jobs are being lost. There will be another mass of unemployed people, just as there was with the revolutions that went before. We will all need to get ahead of the curve. . .

These are just some of the red flags raised by the Information Revolution. Yet, it can't be denied that data can be analysed and processed faster than was ever possible in human history. Information can be collated and used to analyse markets, build conceptual models of intricate systems. It can be used to model new inventions, design buildings. With the internet, more and more data is available, and information can be shared more easily than ever before. It means that, today, someone sitting anywhere in the world who has access to the internet is able to plug themselves into vast amounts of knowledge. No longer is learning limited to the classroom. It is now available to the whole world.

The Educational Revolution that is in motion

On the back of the Information Revolution, I believe the Educational Revolution is in motion. It has already started. And in this Revolution, opportunities will open for everyone.

Education is vital for the many problems the world faces.

The way people learn, and what they are taught in schools is very much the same as it was in the 19th century. When is the curriculum going to catch up with what really needs to be taught, such as balancing a budget, how to manage your money, how to think or be in tune with your mental health? Mindfulness, entrepreneurship, healthy eating, communication skills, the mental side of exercise and sports are all subjects that can be taught, but which are completely overlooked in the classical education system. Then there are other matters, such as respecting other people's boundaries and beliefs, awareness of diversity, relationships, friends, networking, sex, social and global issues, global warming, plastic and recycling—and so much more.

For me, this is one of the reasons my industry is so appealing. It continues to grow because more and more people are seeking to learn things that help us become the best versions of ourselves far beyond where school let us down. People are keen on learning how to find love, become more confident, increase their self-esteem, learn yoga, mindfulness, NLP, public speaking skills, how to become happier, learn marketing, make money, build a property portfolio, and become a more complete and rounded human being.

So around the world, millions of people are attending seminars, viewing YouTube and learn something new. At the time this book is being published:

- 300 hours of video are uploaded to YouTube every minute.

- Almost 5 billion videos are watched on YouTube every single day.

- Self-improvement represents a $10 billion per year industry in the USA alone.

- $300 MILLION is the revenue generated by the 2006 self-help book and DVD *The Secret.*

- The book reached the top of the *New York Times* bestseller list, and remained there for 146 consecutive weeks.

- E-Learning was valued at $165 billion in 2015. It is estimated to be $240 billion in 2023, with 5 per cent growth per annum.

- The wellness industry is worth $3 trillion

- 5 PER CENT—the average annual growth of the personal development market, which far exceeds global economic trends.

- 15 MILLION COPIES—Dale Carnegie is often said be the father of the personal development industry with his famous book *How to Win Friends and Influence People.* First published in 1936, it went on to sell over 15 million copies and is still a bestseller.

- 20 MILLION—the number of copies Stephen Covey's 1989 classic *The Seven Habits of Highly Effective People* has sold to date.

- 45,000 TITLES—the estimated number of self-help books in print.

- Tony Robbins' 'I am not your Guru' is one of the most-watched personal development events on Netflix.

I have been to countless personal development seminars and seen the way education occurs at them. Accelerated learning and using people's emotions as well as their intellects enables people to learn more quickly, makes them motivated to learn more and curious to go further. With technology to help, we have only just started the Educational Revolution!

Our Responsibility

What can be done with education? Far more than we have done so far. I believe we all hold a responsibility to change the world. Parents, educators, inspirers, authors, thinkers hold the key to global change, and we should band together and use technology to encourage real, positive change. We can't leave it to the teachers, politicians or the governments in charge of education. We have the technology and the freedom to promote new ideas and give people more opportunities and chances than ever before.

Children in developing countries who are given access to the internet become connected to the outside world and take in new ideas. Some of those ideas are not good; some are simply advertising for large corporations, some are actively destructive.

I believe that if we care about the future of the world and believe in people developing and going further in life, then we should add our potent voices to the mix. We have to get out there and deal with the big issues affecting the world— spreading change with an undeniably positive message. That then, is a revolution in education, for the whole world!

Be honest. . . Are you afraid of change?

Successful people usually relish change—and when they don't relish it, they at least get what change is going to mean to them.

Some understand that change is going to be uncomfortable simply because they are going to new places. That's the nature of learning—everything we have ever done for the first time will feel *different—uncomfortable—strange*. After a while it becomes normal and then it becomes a habit. So if you are going to have habits, learn new things that are good for you. Have good habits.

If you are looking to grow, evolve, develop, learn, find, seek, create, optimise, enhance, inspire, help, show, boost, turbo-charge, believe, you MUST welcome change. You must see it as a natural part of life.

The question is simple, either you want to be a part of the revolution, or you want to be left behind.

You can fear change, or you can embrace it and use it to your advantage. Becoming stuck in a single idea means you'll end up on the losing side of history. But what if you are afraid of change? Really, genuinely afraid? There are ways to deal with it.

The Questions to ask yourself:

What revolution is going to happen in your life?

What have you been holding back on?

What decisions do you need to make, now?

How great will your life be once you have come out on the other side?

Seven ways to Welcome the Necessary Revolutions in Your Life

1. Admit your fear.

   It's important that you recognise your fear for what it is. Many people deny they're afraid of something, they hide it, they lie to themselves, acknowledge what scares them. They fear the consequences of change. Sometimes you hear people say they aren't *afraid*, but that they *hate* something. But you don't hate something for its own sake. The Ancient Greeks were clear about this—hatred is born of fear. You hate it because you are afraid of what it stands for and the change it will bring to your life.

2. Understand your fear.

   It's worth asking the question of your fear—is it really true?

   Look at it more closely. Many people find that by studying something and understanding its motives or what it really means, they realise they misunderstood it. Sometimes they are lacking information or have a distorted view of what the change in their lives might mean.

When you ask this question, seek the counter examples, the things that show you might be wrong.

Once you've found them and understood the change from lots of different directions, then you can balance them against each other. You might realise you only had a partial understanding of what the change means, or generalised it, so you imagined that one bad aspect of the change meant all the change would be bad.

But remember—this means being brave. You have to be absolutely honest with yourself and really engage with it.

3. Reframe.

Look at reframing and re-understanding the change you fear. You might well find that by looking at something in a fresh light, you see a whole new way to deal with it.

A famous king once tried to turn the tide back by commanding it to do so. King Canute sat in his throne, so the story goes, and soon the tide overran him and he nearly drowned.

Two completely different frames attach to this story.

One says this was evidence of the king's arrogance in trying to command the sea.

A reframe of the story says the king was demonstrating his humility, by proving to his subjects that even he couldn't control the tide, that it was under God's command.

Remember—if you can't stop the tide, find a new way to understand it!

4. Look for ways to make change your friend.

What's the best that can happen when the change you fear comes along? Is it really as bad as all that? How do you make change your friend? How do you make it useful to you? If it's inevitable, then what do you need to do to make your life the best you possibly can—and live well with change? What are the best points about change?

5. What's going on with you?

Is your fear real, or is it that you have an emotional attachment to the way things are now that simply doesn't stack up? If you like the way things are because 'that's how they've always been', does that mean you're actually being lazy? Should you give yourself a kick in the pants and work out what stops you accepting the change?

6. What's the worst and what's the best that could happen?

Planning ahead and seeing how things might work out gives you the opportunity to be prepared. You should aim for the thing that is the very best outcome—and at the same time, insulate yourself however you can from the worst things. Taking stock of what might happen and working out different scenarios is going to give you an advantage. It means you've got an answer.

7. Reinvent yourself.

Find new ways to be that will accommodate the new story you are telling. Make yourself see your situation in a new frame and seek the opportunities. You might well find that in this reinvention, you turn out to be king! For more about reinvention, read on

Reinvention—A Better You

There will come a time when you look at your life and realise that the things you have been doing aren't working for you anymore. I have interviewed and met many people who have had a 'Turning Point' in their lives. That might be for any number of reasons. It might be that the world has changed and your business model doesn't apply any more. It might be that you are bored with what you are doing. Maybe you have hit rock bottom, maybe you are looking for something new in your life, a new challenge or direction.

This is no bad thing. Remember what I said earlier about success? For some successful people, dissatisfaction is what pushes them on. Such people are always finding new ways and new angles to get more from life, to create and meet new challenges.

Whatever the reason—disaster, revolution or a new resolution—it's time to reinvent yourself.

Reinvention comes in two main forms. Some carry on doing what they were already doing at core but find new ways to express it—better ways, different ways. They don't change their main roles, but change how they do it—these I call the Chameleons.

There are those who start again from scratch in a completely new area of life—these I call the Transformers.

I've been both in my time.

The Chameleons

David Bowie was one of those enigmatic characters with a determination to succeed. As a teenager in the 1960s, he announced that he was going to be a rock star, before he could even play an instrument. The following decade saw him experimenting with which instruments were right for him. He started off as a sax player. When he realised that singing while playing sax would be impossible, he switched to guitar. He tried numerous different approaches to songwriting, doing serious songs, ballads in different styles and even writing a comedy record, 'The Laughing Gnome'.

It was only in 1969, with his single 'Space Oddity', that people began to pay attention to him. Yet he'd been around in the music business by then for years—reinventing himself continually.

Over the course of his career, he reinvented himself over and over. From Major Tom, to Ziggy Stardust, to Aladdin Sane to The Thin White Duke and beyond, David Bowie was a Chameleon who changed his colours but remained at core the same thing—a rock singer. Of course, he also acted, wrote and painted—but at his core he was one thing.

Numerous others have done the same thing. Madonna is famed for reinventing her look and her style repeatedly. Picasso started off as a precise painter of lifelike portraits, and then created his own unique style of painting that was a complete departure from where he began.

Billionaire businessman Lord Alan Sugar has done this, too. His 'thing' was that he always wanted to trade. He started when he was a young boy by selling tar-soaked wood dug up from the roads in London to be used as fire-lighters. He got into making and selling hi-fi systems in the 1970s, then invented his own cheap tower systems under the name of Amstrad in the 1980s.

With each change and each revolution in the marketplace, Lord Sugar adapted. When computers started to change the entire home electronics marketplace in the 1980s, he was there—designing and introducing his own brand of PC. When the hard drives he was using turned out to be faulty and the company made a loss, he had a fire sale and reinvented the business as a satellite dish manufacture— finally selling it to Sky for £125 million.

He has continued as a serial entrepreneur, because his major skill is in seeing opportunities and selling things. More recently, he has also hosted the TV show *The Apprentice*. Yes, he's now a TV personality, but his core skill is in sales, and that never changed, though he reinvented his interests repeatedly.

Lord Sugar is another of the great chameleons—reinventors, whose business products change but who at core remain the same.

The Transformers

Though there is sometimes overlap between the Chameleons and the Transformers, the latter group are the ones who change their lives completely, and carry on.

Harrison Ford was one such Transformer. Having worked in the Hollywood studio system in the 1960s, Ford realised his career was going nowhere. He was a slave to the system and one of the bosses at Universal simply didn't like him. Harrison had a choice—to continue doing the same thing, which included being a failed actor, or doing something completely different.

When a friend said he wanted a table built for his home, Harrison offered to make it. He had no skill in carpentry, but he decided to get books out from the library and simply follow the instructions. Within a few months, he was getting calls for jobs on a regular basis and making good money.

What difference did this complete change in career make to his life? Harrison still wanted to act, but he was now able to go to auditions with a renewed sense of confidence. He wasn't completely reliant on the outcome of the audition, and this allowed him to relax. That's when he landed a role in George Lucas's *American Graffiti*.

This wasn't, however, the start of his rise to mega-stardom. Harrison was having the wild time he had always dreamed he would have as a younger man, and at one drinks party had a fight with co-star Richard Dreyfuss, throwing him off a second floor hotel balcony into the swimming pool. At that point, George Lucas decided he would never work with him again.

That's why he wasn't called for a new role Lucas was casting. Instead, his agent got him building a door into the building that Lucas walked through every morning for the auditions. Richard Dreyfuss also came to that audition, but didn't get the role.

Lucas couldn't find the right actor. The auditions went on for weeks. Finally Lucas relented and invited Harrison to audition. That was when he landed his role as Han Solo—a role that took him to mega-stardom.

Harrison Ford's transformation as a carpenter was short-lived—but it was this complete change that literally opened a new door for him.

Other Transformers include J K Rowling, whose life as a teacher in Portugal fell apart after she separated from her abusive partner. She ended up writing in Edinburgh. The life of the expat she had enjoyed in sunny Portugal was exchanged for a life in cold Scotland. It was a complete revolution in her life, which saw her at her lowest ebb, a single mother living on benefits.

Yet J K Rowling took the opportunity to write the book she believed in, *Harry Potter and the Philosopher's Stone*, and followed her heart, reinventing herself as a novelist. As it turned out, she became the most successful novelist of modern times.

A fascinating and deeply inspiring figure is that of Nick Vujicic. Nick was born with tetra-amelia, meaning he has only residual limbs instead of fully formed arms and legs. He spent his early years angry at the world for his disability and contemplated committing suicide at the age of eight.

One day when he was 17, his mother showed him an article about a man with a severe disability who was making the most of his life. It had a transformational effect on Nick, who decided he would stop being angry and instead be grateful for all the good things in his life. He began to give motivational talks at his local church. Soon, word spread about his inspirational attitude to life. Nick has gone on to spread his message of hope to millions through books, DVDs, TV shows and inspirational talks. He now has a wife and two kids. For him, his success comes from the heart, and is the product of a strong spiritual belief and sense of personal mission to spread good news to the world.

I'll talk more about attitude and gratitude again, later.

What Reinvention Is Not

When the word reinvention comes up, sometimes people think it means they should pluck a persona from the air that isn't true to who they are. Reinvention is not about suddenly becoming someone else—it's the opposite. It's about becoming more the person you really are, by using the opportunity of reinvention to find new sides of yourself that have long been hidden.

When you reinvent yourself, it doesn't have to be as the result of a revolution, of suddenly feeling lost or dislocated from your former life—though for some people that is what's needed to shake them from their comfortable lives into one that's more meaningful. Maybe it's just that you need to become your 2.0 version. Maybe you just want to become healthier, fitter, funnier, find love. All these things, too, are reinvention.

Change or reinvention is not necessarily a mid-life crisis.

I am not a big fan of these words, used too often by people around you. In particular, friends and loved ones might see 'the new' you as a mid-life crisis, but I recommend you live your life around your reality, not theirs. Be a bit 'selfish'. Why not?

* * *

THE QUESTION:
Do you think it might be too late for you?

IT IS NEVER TOO LATE. NEVER!

* * *

Richard Bandler talks about how we have the latest phone devices, we download the latest software, or buy the latest models of computers and TVs, but we expect to improve in life without updating ourselves. If you think it's too late, think again. Many, many people have made profound changes much later in life. Here are just a few, but remember—you are surrounded by change and reinvention.

- Morgan Freeman had his first Hollywood role at 52.

- Ray Kroc used to drive around the US selling milkshake machines. When he was 52, he met Maurice and Richard McDonald, and the McDonald's franchise was born.

- Andrea Bocelli began his professional opera career at 34, after working as a lawyer.

- JRR Tolkien was a successful university professor who wrote little-known works. The Hobbit was published when he was 43. His next fiction book, The Lord of the Rings came out when he was 62.

- Trevor Bayliss was a swimming pool salesman, swimmer and stuntman. Then, at the age of 48, he began inventing aids for the disabled. He was 55 when he filed his first patent for the clockwork radio, which sold in its millions. A successful inventor, he went on to mentor other inventors.

- Sylvester Stallone was broke and didn't become successful until 30, when he created the role for the movie *Rocky*.

- Jon Hamm spent years auditioning unsuccessfully and waiting tables until he landed the role of Don Draper in *Mad Men* at the age of 36.

Seven ways to Reinvent Yourself and Find Your Calling in Life

Though many people dream of a different future, we often spend much of our life focusing on what needs to be done closer to hand. It's part of most people's make-up to spend their energies on what is most likely to affect them now. That's why change so often comes with unexpected upheaval. But you can make changes and go after your goal without being prompted by a disaster.

When we do go for change, we often quit before seeing our dreams through to the end—which requires understanding what we need to do and the steps along the way to reinventing ourselves, changing our expectations and attitudes as life goes by—and upgrading them!

1. Look out for the rut.

   Be aware of what you're doing every day. If you don't make at least some contribution to your long term plan once a day, then you will not find it easy to move forwards. Writers will often set themselves a minimum word count to write every day. People saving up money will make sure a certain amount is put aside every week. There has to be something beyond doing your emails and catching up on tv shows or whatever makes your particular 'rut'. Otherwise you'll get nowhere.

2. Know what you want.

It helps to find out what you want for your future by taking yourself there in your imagination. One exercise that helps with this is to see yourself as an older person.

What do you want it to be like?

What do you see around you?

A loving family?

A lonely room?

Wealth and comfort?

Do you see yourself satisfied when helping others?

Do you feel regrets for the things you didn't do?

That last question is a strong indicator of what you should be striving for!

Remember, too, that seeing yourself in your ideal future is a strong psychological incentive to getting there. Visualisation of yourself enjoying your future life will help you along the way. There's a hint you might want to take on board here, which means you are more likely to succeed. If you say to yourself: 'I'm going to be a genius concert pianist,' that's fantastic—but it's a big chunk and a huge leap. If you tell yourself: 'To get there, every day I'm going to practise the piano and get better', you are focusing on the process of continual improvement. That's something that, provided you do it, you can't fail at! It's a process goal rather than an outcome goal—but one that will support you on the way to the final outcome you want.

Check also that the outcome is what you really want and that it is achievable. Remember: 'defying gravity' or 'turning back the tide' may not be realistic outcomes!

3. Know thyself.

It's vital to know yourself. Remember what I said about being honest? You have to be as honest as you can with yourself, all of the time.

Take some time to think over your life. Find how your passions are ignited in the world and see how you can connect with them.

The Questions to ask yourself:

What are you capable of?

Where are you strong?

When are you super amazing?

Where are you weak? Be honest!

What ignites your passions?

Ask yourself, too, are your future plans what you want, or are you being overly influenced by people who have a different agenda? Sometimes, outside pressure can make you lose sight of your own goals and values.

Sometimes it's easy to lie to yourself because you don't have a complete picture of who you are, what your strengths are and what you are capable of. Be brutally honest, and ask trusted friends to be brutally honest, too. Discussions with trusted advisers and mentors can really help you understand who you are and what you can do. You might surprise yourself!

4. Be aware of the task in hand.

It's all too easy to imagine it's going to be easy. People who get excited and inspired by the grand vision of what their new life will be like often overlook the complexity of each step along the way. When you know what you want to achieve, work your way backwards, working out what you want to achieve before that and before that, until you get to the place you're in now. Visualise each step along the way. This trains you to know what to expect. Anticipate difficulties so you can meet them, so you don't have to improvise all the time. Have strategies to hand to deal with obstacles along the way, but also don't over-focus on difficulties. Keep them in proportion and be ready for them as you strive toward your goal.

You can do that by talking with people who've already been there. It's amazing how generous many people are with their expertise. They want to see other people succeed. Ask experts. Get a mentor and get the reality beyond the dream.

5. Create new habits.

    To get where you want to go, you will need to create new habits. This can be time-consuming and energy-depleting at the beginning. It requires a change in mental attitude if you want to learn a new skill, get fitter through exercise or eat different foods.

    If you say to yourself, 'I would like to travel more', that is going to lead to inertia because there isn't a piece of activity attached to it. If you say to yourself instead, 'I'm going to book at least one trip a month', and you then ensure that you set aside a time to look at your options, price up travel and set time aside for the travel itself, you are much more likely to actually get out the door. Committing to leaving on a trip once a month is a much more useful aim than the vague 'I'll travel more'.

    Of course, this requires recognising the time it will take to do—so be straight with yourself and factor in the extra time. You know it makes sense.

    I recommend you to read *The Power of Habit: Why We Do What We Do*, by Charles Duhigg.

6. Work with others.

    You don't have to work alone. By spending time in a club, group or association of like-minded people, you are far more likely to succeed in what you want on your journey to reinvention. I have received amazing advice and inspiration from the mentoring groups I have joined in the past, made really useful connections that made a massive difference in my life—and made highly valued friends, too.

7. Measure, assess, celebrate

Check how you are doing, where you've actually got to, against the goals you have set yourself.

The Questions to ask yourself:

Am I moving forward?

Am I closer to achieving what I want to achieve thanks to my actions?

Am I closer to leaving a legacy?

This will help keep you motivated. Set aside time to do that.

If your assessment says that you aren't getting there, reassess what you want to achieve and the methods you've chosen to get there. This way you get to fine-tune repeatedly.

This is extremely good for the soul.

When you do see your goal closer, or your pass a marker, then celebrate.

Recognise the moments of joy your path is bringing you and give gratitude for it. That is how to keep yourself emotionally engaged.

Then. . . go on for more of the same!

That's it.

Now, what's stopping you?

Nothing?

Go for it.

Chapter 4

YOU AND YOUR SURROUNDINGS

This is the part where we focus on building you. We've read about the amazing stories of our ancestors and how they pushed the boundaries and have created the most amazing things for us. We've looked into what greatness and success is and the three pillars to success.

So in order to move forward, let's look at you and what might be holding you back. The Questions to ask yourself:

Are you fit?

Do you take care of yourself?

Do you appreciate the importance of eating well and exercising?

Are you being honest?

Are you thinking properly?

Your Body

The Journey Ahead

You're stepping out on a journey to make amazing changes in your life. You're going to experience new things, meet new people and encounter new ideas. Part of preparing for the journey ahead is to make sure that you are fit to do it. And the benefits of fitness for your mind and your physical wellbeing are massive.

With fitness you get focus; with the right foods nourishing your brain and your body you get better results. With better blood supply to you brain, endorphins in your body, your mood will be buoyed, you will be doing different things and thinking in new ways. This change in itself is a start for getting rid of old habits.

So, this section is going to ask the basic questions about you and your life.

The Questions to ask yourself:

How can I become better?

What food should I eat?

Should I eat less?

Should I try fasting?

What exercise should I do?

Have I even been or felt fit?

How did it feel?

Have I given up?

You do understand how eating the wrong food, abusing alcohol or sugary drinks can kill you or substantially reduce your lifespan, don't you?

I'm going to make some suggestions and ask some questions. And I want you to answer them honestly.

The Question: Are you as fit as you would like to be?

Make an assessment of your body and mind.

Do you feel tired in the morning when you wake up?

Do feel like you carry too much weight?

Do you feel your movement is restricted due to lack of exercise?

Can you imagine how much better you would feel were you to exercise and eat better?

Do you want to try new things in food and exercise?

If the answer to *any* of these questions is 'yes', then it's time to consider what to do about your fitness. Now!

* * *

1. Exercise—The First Step.

When you're fitter and stronger, it's not just your body that works better. Your mind works better, your mental health improves and your ability to focus, to think and make decisions gets better, too. If exercise is already part of your life, great. Ask yourself—is it enough? How could I take my fitness to the next level? Are there other things I would like to try? What do I get from exercise? For example, a run or a workout can energise, while yoga can calm and focus. Try new things to see how they add to your level of fitness and the tools you have for being you.

That said, if you're not someone who exercises much and you are looking for a start on the journey to the best you, it's time to step out, literally.

The following is a recommendation for people who've let exercise go and are starting from a base of very little experience with exercise. The principles, however, are the same for everyone at any level.

We're constantly advised to exercise more, yet many find squeezing it into busy schedules a chore. For others, gym membership or keeping fitness equipment doesn't fit their lifestyle. So what's to be done to get that fitness level raised, the heart beating faster and wellbeing flooding through mind and body—in a fun, enjoyable experience?

To start with, let's look at the benefits of something that's as easy to do as putting one foot in front of the other. No excuses, please!

Walking can be a fascinating and enjoyable way of getting to know the place you live, of enjoying the countryside, of exploring any new area and meeting people. Simply getting out into daylight and raising the heart rate can have hugely beneficial effects. In a recent study, the British Heart Foundation discovered that people who walk briskly for half an hour a day can reduce the risk of heart attack by up to 40 per cent.

Meanwhile, another study showed that coming into contact with nature, as you do on a country walk, powerfully reduces stress levels. The secret ingredient, scientists say, is the greenery around you. There's even a name for not coming into contact with nature enough—'nature deficit disorder'.

But that's not all. The steady rhythm of walking can also have a powerful positive effect on the mind. Many people talk about needing to go for a walk to clear their heads, and there is much to it.

The effect of regular rhythm on the mind can be extremely useful for people wishing to marshal their thoughts. None other than the great poet William Wordsworth found it a powerful tonic to help him compose poems. His walks through his native Lakeland countryside as a boy are well recorded, as is his 2000-mile walk through Europe during the French Revolution.

Throughout his life, Wordsworth continued to pace to help him to write, finding that the rhythm of his stride repeated itself in the rhythm of his poems. It has been estimated that Wordsworth must have walked 180,000 miles in his life—and it did him good, living as he did to the grand old age of 80.

The focusing and calming effect of walking has been taken to its extreme in the meditations of Buddhists, who use the steady rhythm to slow the mind and disentangle it from the 'veil of illusion' they see as the cause of human suffering. Walking meditation is used by many Buddhists to get to mindfulness—a calm and relaxed awareness that is detached from deep emotions.

Whether you walk for fitness, for enjoyment or sociability, for nature appreciation—or to write that masterpiece— the great advantage of walking is that you just have to get outside your door. Of course, it is wonderful to walk in the countryside, but a decent pair of shoes and the appropriate clothes mean you can enjoy this health-giving pastime wherever you are.

Or if you are working at a desk, like Wordsworth in his later years, you might just want to pace your room, controlling and directing your thoughts as easily as you direct your feet.

So, the next time you consider jumping in the car to take that short five-minute journey, think again.

And now I'm going to use one of those personal development clichés we hear everywhere, but is still useful:

A journey of a thousand miles begins with a single step.

(But several thousand steps are better!)

* * *

Walking Facts

Composer J S Bach once walked 260 miles to hear Buxtehude, a famous organist, play. More remarkably, this 20-year-old composer then walked back weighed down with manuscript copies he had made of the organist's playing.

Walking that raises the heart rate is good for the heart and for stamina, while walking with care and attention, with a slow, steady movement, is helpful to building mental stamina.

The great thing about walking is that it is free—and walking in the countryside is known to have positive effects on mood and mental wellbeing.

* * *

A Few More Famous Walkers.

Aristotle, the famed Greek philosopher, gave lectures while walking. His (quite literally) *followers* were known as the peripatetics—a Greek word for walking about.

Charles Dickens used to write from 9 in the morning until the early afternoon and then finished with a long walk, often of up to 30 miles! At nights, plagued with insomnia, he'd walk through London's streets, often gaining inspiration for stories.

Albert Einstein often took a long walk on the beach to introspect and work out complex problems in his head.

(I personally love walking. It really helps me think more clearly; it also helps me when I want to come up with ideas. I find it really helpful.)

Getting the Exercise that is Right for You

Whatever exercise you choose to do, do your research first and make sure it's the right thing for you. Of course, if you have joint pains, or restrictions on movement, then maybe it's another exercise you need to consider. Remember, there are ways around the problems that hold you back!

If you are heavy, then running may put strain and wear on your joints. Swimming may be a better option; it's also an excellent exercise for people who can't have high impact on their joints. Cycling is great for maintaining focus, again without high impact. If you are sight impaired, then you may need to have someone come with you, or you might go to a spinning class, where you don't have to worry about being out on the road. Getting out and about and enjoying yourself with others is also part of the pay-off for exercise. Consider joining a club or group that exercises regularly—it may be exactly what you need for your mind, too.

If you haven't exercised for many years, then your muscles and tendons will need to strengthen before you go into more energetic training. Getting blood flowing to your muscles and tendons will make your body strengthen those parts of your body you have neglected. You've got to upgrade the machinery of your body first before you can take on greater levels of exercise.

2. Mind and Body

Focusing on mind and body together will also pay off in different ways. Many people find that stress in their lives is relieved by exercises like yoga and t'ai chi. The steady concentration on slow movements, breath control and stretching can encourage a sense of wellbeing that is highly effective. Pilates is another favourite; chi kung, or for something completely different, climbing, can also have extraordinarily positive effects on concentration as well as physical strength and poise.

For fun, juggling and circus skills might be the thing for you. There is a whole world of physicality out there for you to explore, and with it will come a new way of thinking about the world, as well as noticeable differences in your mental wellbeing.

There are plenty of resources for you to look up.

The Questions to ask yourself:

What stops you? How do you get beyond any blocks to what is good for you?

Yoga—A Case Study

There is a fascinating and deeply inspiring video that you can find on YouTube that tells the story of Arthur Boorman, a US war veteran who was crippled in the Gulf War and was told by doctors he would never walk unassisted again.

For 15 years Boorman listened to their advice, gaining weight and living a limited, unhappy life. But then, at the age of 47 Boorman discovered DDP yoga and began to train. The YouTube video traces his steady recovery as he learned to retrain his muscles to compensate for his injuries. He was 297 pounds when he started, and within 10 months had shed 140 pounds, was able to perform incredible feats with yoga, and to run unassisted.

His life was completely transformed.

Yoga has also been used to calm the mind and treat PTSD in soldiers, and is a powerful tool for treating depression and addiction.

There are many types of yoga, each with different emphases. From traditional Hatha, Kripalu, Kundalini, Iyengar through to more modern Hot Yoga, Power Yoga and Rocket Yoga, there will be a form that will suit most people.

The discipline began in ancient India, probably around the 5th and 6th centuries BCE, and has an emphasis on spiritual, physical and mental practices. In the modern world as it has come to the West, some forms of yoga have emphasised the power and physicality of the discipline, while others build on the spiritual. That it has a powerful effect on the mind and body cannot be doubted, with many people reporting more focus, more happiness and an ability to handle stress, while also feeling physically stronger, more supple and more flexible.

It's one suggestion out of the many, many things you can try. What stops you giving it a go?

3. Eating Right

There's an old saying that you are what you eat. And of course, it is literally true. Let me be blunt: the size of your mouth is a lot bigger than your arsehole! Remember, you have to burn what you eat, you have to sweat, speed up your metabolism and kick-start it into burning off calories!!

The food you eat is taken into your body to make you who you are. If you eat things cooked with lots of oil, fried, or with lots of sugar and salt, and you eat more than you burn, well you know what's going to happen. It isn't rocket science.

Don't care right now? You know you will at some point!

Is failing to look after yourself and failing to ensure your body is well and fit something you want to regret later?

It's not worth it. My advice is: *take action, now!*

This section is not a detailed look at nutrition, but it is worth discussing several different approaches to eating, and what you put in your body.

The first thing to note is that most people eat too much and have too much sugar.

I think one of the problems with the way the West has come to regard food is that it falls into two main conceptual categories. It is either seen as fuel, or it is seen as a drug that acts as a substitute for the things that are really missing from your life.

And while it is true that food is what fuels us, it's not true to say that it's *only* a fuel. Over thousands of years, food has become as much a social and spiritual entity as it is something to put into your body. Over millennia, different cultures have made food central to human identity. From the pride of lions eating gathered round a fresh kill on the African savannah, through to the great apes who sit in groups, eating food they have picked or caught (because yes, some apes are carnivores) and removing fleas and ticks from the hair and skin of other community members, to the celebration of food in religious rituals, which recognise the social importance of food, food has always had a strong social element.

The Holy Sacrament is one such ritual that has its social side overlooked, and yet the supper that it celebrates is the mythical presentation of a coming together of friends before great changes were to take place. Throughout history, food is used as a symbol that says that people are spiritually united through the food they eat. This is just one example of the way food has a wider significance than simply being fuel.

To this day in rural parts of France, towns and villages close down for two hours so that people can take the time to eat together. Food is an integral part of society and social well-being—it is good for the spirit because it draws people together and they share each other's company. During such times, happiness-creating chemicals are released in people's brains—not just by the food, but by the company they keep. Coming together to eat is a social good, far beyond food itself.

When such attitudes are undermined, that is when food becomes a drug. An unhappy individual, divorced from the everyday connections of the world, seeks to find ways to fill the void, to recreate the missing feelings of wellbeing no longer provided by social interaction. Binge-ing on foods—especially fats and sugars—gives a quick hit to the nervous system that takes away the pain for a while. But the emptiness of such a use of food feeds on itself—leaving a lonely person more lonely and, because they're piling on weight, more unhappy than before.

Food, then, isn't just something to use in different ways, either as a fuel or as a drug. It is part of the shape of your life. It shapes you, in more ways than one. And that's why, although losing weight and a well-balanced diet are both good things, they are nowhere near as good as getting a well-balanced life in which food plays its part.

This is the problem with the countless diets and fads on the market at the moment. And not only with the diets, but also with that one question many people have in rela-tion to food: 'How do I lose weight?'

Late in my life I have started fasting. My son Lucci and some friends of mine started looking into the Keto diet, which mainly consists of fasting for long hours, cutting down to two meals and not eating a lot of carbs, and I have to say I haven't felt better in my life. The level of energy I have, and even more the mental clarity I have, is like I have never experienced before.

Yes, losing weight is important for your wellbeing and health, but it is only part of your direction of travel. That, I hope, will be to find a happy and fulfilling life, which means you don't think of food merely as a mechanical need or as a drug, but as something that is part of your whole, happy, successful life.

Your Mind

As well as your body, there's also your mind. It's time to go deep and look more closely at how your psychology affects you and your universe—and the skills you need to use your mind well and wisely.

Let's look at:

1. Honesty

2. Ego

3. Your breathing and how it affects your brain processes

4. How you think

5. How to change your thoughts

6. The power of visualisation

7. The law of attraction

8. Gratitude

1. Honesty—The Roots of the Tree

Is honesty a rare commodity now? In an age of fake news and secrecy, sometimes it can feel that way. It seems people struggle to be honest and don't even value the idea of honesty.

Do you ever think that *honesty* can be an empty word?

Do you think sometimes it can be paradoxical?

In the West we tend to struggle to be totally, authentically honest. We prefer to use white lies instead of upsetting someone with the truth.

In my experience, people often say they are looking for honesty but can't seem to deal with it when they get it. People often ask for my opinion, but before I answer I normally make sure they really want honest feedback. I like being straightforward. I say things how I see them. That can cause problems.

A friend of mine summed up the outcome of my approach with the famous hashtag—#SorryNotSorry. She was right. Because though I may be sorry if I upset someone (and it is never my intention to do so), I'm also not sorry, because good friends are honest with each other. Good friends say things that need to be said.

Honesty is the root to the tree, the water for the plant, the sun for the earth. It's how we learn, grow and change.

For people who really want change in their lives, honesty with yourself is absolutely the most important thing to have, before anything else. To be honest with others, first be honest with yourself.

When you use evasion, avoidance and misdirection to protect yourself from hard questions and even harder answers, you're letting your ego get in the way. Ask yourself, why are you scared of being honest? How can you use honesty to make positive change in your life?

Dishonesty isn't always deliberate. Maybe you aren't even aware of how dishonest you are with yourself. When you look at yourself in the mirror and you are not happy with what you see, what do you do?

Do you change the subject and think of something else?

Or do you ask yourself a set of questions:

*   *   *

The Questions that Need an Honest Answer

Take as much time as you need to answer these as fully as possible.

Am I honest with others?

Can I handle the truth?

Am I happy with the way things are?

What do I want that is different from now?

How do I get that different thing instead of this?

What is the first thing I need to do to make that happen?

Do I keep coming up with excuses?

Am I willing to take responsibility for the things in my control?

Do I believe I'm going to do it?

If not, what stops me?

How do I overcome objections and obstacles?

With those objections and obstacles met, what else stops me?

If nothing, than when am I going to act? (Hint: NOW).

*   *   *

The Questions above are useful for all sorts of problems. If you have not been happy for a while, use them to get to the next stage—which is making happiness happen. They will help you change what is going on now!

With this kind of implacable self-questioning you cannot hide from yourself any more. You can't protect your fragile ego from awkward facts. We will be going in a bit deeper into the ego next, but for now, once you've asked yourself these questions and got honest answers, you know it's time to act.

'But,' you might object. 'what if I don't have the answers?'

Sure, you could think like that. Let's be clear. You can see questions as a test that you either pass or fail, like you used to see them at school, or you can see them as tools to check where you have knowledge that is useful, and where you need to find knowledge—which is what those questions at school were originally asked for.

The questions to yourself above are the starting points for finding answers.

Without them, you have nothing to motivate you because you don't even know what you're looking for.

With them, you've got a launchpad for finding the answers. So start looking.

* * *

The Question: So, what do I do if I don't have the answer?
Answer: So many things. Start looking. Start asking around. Research. Ask for advice.

* * *

Sometimes you're going to need help. Ask a friend, seek out a guide, find a mentor. Look for people who can guide you. Find out who can help you. You do not have to face questions you can't answer alone. You don't have to do it all alone. That also is an answer.

Because you are wise, you will know what you need to do and who to find. First, make yourself open to receiving help. Your unconscious also needs to ask the universe for guidance. Guidance will come if you acknowledge that you want it.

Remember: Honesty is what you need to move forward, so, no more lies. If you think it's time to make the changes you want, then you've got to promise yourself and me that you won't lie to yourself or hide from the answers any more.

Is that a deal?

* * *

Now give yourself time to ask what you want to change in your life. Take some time out. Ask yourself the hard questions. And then commit, in your head, to me and to you that from now on you'll always be straight with yourself and deal with the answers you seek, passionately and unflinchingly being true to yourself!

And remember—though asking the right questions is a starting point, answering your questions positively is the only way to go.

The answer to 'What do I want?' is not 'I want to stop. . . / I don't want to. . .'

You need an answer that sets a positive direction. Something you can do, not something you can 'not do'.

With these first answers, there will be more questions. Honesty is your resource to face the exciting changes and challenges ahead. Use it.

* * *

2. Ego

We hear a lot about the word *Ego*. 'He's got such a big ego... he's an egomaniac'. We think about artists and actors having egos that are out of control. But everyone has an ego, and it can be a tough cookie to deal with, because—

your ego is your identity. It's who you think you are.

Different theories exist about whether the ego exists and what the ego is for. Some say the ego has a negative role to play in your life and you should try to get rid of it to go toward a spiritual goal. On the other hand, some scientists say it is vital to maintain for mental health.

In old-fashioned psychology, the ego is often presented as the conscious, reality-driven part of yourself that appears to be logical and realistic, but is actually responding to deep instinctual and emotional drives.

Eastern philosophy has its own way of looking at ego. Buddhism, for example, has a similar concept, which it terms Anatta—and just like in the West, it really means 'the illusion of the self'.

Why an illusion? Because it is only what you think your 'self' is. It's conscious, it's rational and seems to put you in control of what you do. Yet that's where the illusion begins, because you don't recognise you are driven by a whole matrix of drives, history, instincts and half-recognised impulses. And it means you are heavily defined by your surroundings and your past.

The philosopher Nietzsche once wrote, 'What a person IS begins to betray itself when his talent decreases—when he ceases to show what he can DO.'

Just so with you. Whatever your talents and skills, they are not who you are. The shopkeeper with no shop is not a shop-keeper and the singer who loses his voice is not a singer. Yet we wrap ourselves in identities that are not who we are.

The habits you have learned from childhood and been conditioned into are exactly that—habits you have picked up. They are not you.

That's why it's vital to go below your conditioning—all the stuff your ego has picked up along the way—to find out who the real you is. The goal is to become your true self, to get beyond false consciousness to who you really are.

Doing so frees so much energy. It makes you joyful and alive in the moment. Being in contact with your real self brings energy, lightness and contentment. You are creative and constructive when you inner self is being expressed freely without being suppressed by expectations you've learned from the world around you. The good, the kind, the great and the generous are born from it.

My own view is we should not try to eradicate the ego. Instead, we perform a balancing act. After all, the ego is also the part of you that thinks, acts, discriminates and decides. The skill, then, is in managing your ego, using it for your purposes, while at the same time being connected to the deeper levels of yourself. That way you can act and think with all the wise information of deeper parts of yourself to guide you.

You want your ego to be strong AND to be flexible. Not to run out of control, but to be able to respond to needs without perceiving a threat or dogmatically refusing to consider new ideas because 'this is not who I am'. It's having a light touch and a wise way of thinking that you are seeking.

Some of that can be achieved by taking time out to meditate or de-stress in some way; to stop the narratives and stories that are shaping your life from taking over. There are ways to do that—and one of them is to watch your breathing, quietly sitting and relaxing. Try it for 20 minutes a day. It's tough at first—but it can have a fantastic effect on helping you detach from the stories you have been telling yourself. Yoga and other meditative exercise have similar effects.

So in my opinion your ego is necessary. It tries to protect us, but it's only by understanding and being conscious of our thoughts—what we truly are and what we are not—that we can find inner peace and the true self.

Control your ego, do not let it control you!

3. Your Breathing

When you focus on your breathing in the style of the Buddhists, sitting comfortably and maintaining a gentle meditative state, it can have powerful psychological and physiological effects.

Scientists have recently discovered the reasons for this, and note how it helps yogis and masters to attain peace and clear thinking. They discovered that breathing through the nose causes stimulation in the brain, and that the steady focus on the rhythm of breathing can help you achieve different levels of brainwave activity.

Slowing your breathing can slow your thinking and allow you to access different states of mind. Breathing from a deeper place in your stomach, rather than chest breathing, can change the way your brain responds.

It's something I've also noticed in NLP when I'm altering my state to get more in touch with my creative side. Being in a relaxed state and breathing right help me when I'm making decisions and considering my future.

So, take some time out to meditate, or just sit quietly and focus your mind gently and quietly on your breathing. It can make a huge difference to your life and the way you operate.

Mastering meditation, like so many worthwhile things in life, takes time and practice. But study after study proves meditation is able to improve your life in many ways, including reducing stress and improving your ability to concentrate. The following meditation exercise is an excellent introduction; try doing it first thing in the morning before breakfast.

Sit on a chair or lie comfortably in a quiet room.

Close your eyes.

Make no effort to control the breath; simply breathe naturally.

Focus your attention on the breath and on how the body moves with each inhalation and exhalation. Notice the movement of your body as you breathe. Simply focus your attention on your breath without controlling its pace or intensity. If your mind wanders, return your focus back to your breath. Maintain this meditation practice for two to three minutes to start with. As you continue to practise, build up for longer periods, to a maximum of 20 minutes.

4. Thinking

When you're in that relaxed meditative state, you will notice that your thoughts begin to change. You will get beyond the stress of the everyday to a more considered state.

Getting in charge of your thinking is absolutely central to taking charge of your life, yet so few people actually spend time thinking about thinking or practise thinking!

'*The mind is everything. What you think you become.*'

—Buddha

What I find interesting is so many people that teach or are open to learn personal development don't really understand the importance of being in control of what you think and how you think.

Many people have no idea that their thoughts set the backdrop to their experience. They take their thinking and the way they think so completely for granted that they think it's reality itself, rather than their own set of habits their ego has got used to.

That's why knowing how you think is vital.

Ask yourself:

What do you most think about?

Are your thoughts positive, are they constructive, or are they negative for you?

Are they helping you get on in life, to get what you want, or sabotaging you?

Are you thinking about that now?

Research has estimated that people have anywhere from 12,000 to 60,000 thoughts every single day. Yet the same research estimates that up to 98 percent of them are exactly the same as the ones they had the day before. These are exactly the habits of mind it's vital to break to get where you want to go. Amazingly, another estimate put as many as 80 per cent of the thoughts people think in a day as negative.

This is why managing your thinking is vital. What you think IS what you become, as the Buddha says.

I have seen massive changes in habit through the extraordinary power of NLP. In numerous training courses, I saw countless changes in habits of thinking, I saw phobia cures brought about quickly, in minutes. And as it turned out, they were not only fast, but long-lasting.

NLP is a study of the way we think. Its name references the way that the brain (neuro) has a code, or language (linguistic) that can be altered (programming).

Put simply, NLP studies the programming language of the mind—and it also shows you how to change it.

To say NLP has changed my life and the life of millions, including many people in the personal development industry, is an understatement. It's also safe to say that many people go through their whole life never becoming aware of their thoughts nor, most importantly, how to manage them or make them become useful.

For many, thinking about how we think is an alien idea. After all, we are not born with or provided in school with a manual on how to think. We simply get on with life, often making the same errors over and again because we were never taught how to think wisely.

NLP is basically the study of successful people, which asks *how do they do what they do?* Much of NLP co-creator Richard Bandler's work helps people think differently and change beliefs that have held people back all their lives. Phobias, lack of confidence and self esteem are just a few of the many areas in which Richard is an expert in generating change.

As Richard puts it:

> *'The way you think determines the way you feel, and the way you feel determines the way you act or behave.'*

5. Changing Your Thinking

The language in which you think is made up of the same inputs that you get from the outside world. Many people think in pictures most of the time, because that is the main input their brain processes. Of course, sounds, smell, taste and touch are also often involved in thinking. Like the way that many people talk to themselves in their own minds: 'oh, shall I have a cup of tea?' or 'where did I put the—?' But these are all modalities of thinking that are drawn from sensory inputs, even though talking to yourself in your own head, or making a picture of a cup of tea are not inputs from out there, but self-generated.

In his classic book *Psycho-Cybernetics*, Dr Maxwell Maltz noted:

> '*Your subconscious cannot tell the difference between a real memory, and a vividly imagined visualization.*'
> —Dr Maxwell Maltz

This means that if you start to change the pictures you create in your head and the voices you speak to yourself in, you will start to think differently. You will respond differently to inputs, because you are not processing in the way you were before.

You might be thinking to yourself that you can't visualise. But if I ask you to imagine the front door of your house or your car, then within a fraction of a second you make a picture of it in your mind. We all visualise, constantly.

When someone has a fear of snakes or spiders, it isn't necessarily the snake itself that causes the fear. You can be afraid of something without it being in the room, which means it's your thoughts that are making the fear, not the thing in itself.

For example, if you are afraid of snakes and I came and stood next to you and told you I had a snake in my bag, you would probably freak out. You haven't seen it in my bag. Where you saw it was in a picture you made in your head. That picture was most likely very big and very real and very close to you.

I have seen countless examples of people with strong phobias and limiting beliefs overcome them quickly with NLP. There are many techniques to make them go. It might be by use of the fast phobia cure, by using what's known in NLP as a *swish pattern* or simply having someone laugh off their fear—but the effect is the same. People's lives are enriched and enhanced.

The change is made by putting you in charge of the pictures in your head. When you make overpowering pictures tiny, far away, monochrome and grainy—suddenly the fear no longer holds the same power it once did.

With phobias and limiting beliefs gone, people are free to do what they want. Limiting beliefs have such a negative impact, constraining people for no other reason than they think they can't succeed at something. By holding limiting beliefs, we impoverish our lives and limit our identities.

Your beliefs can either be true or false, but if you believe them, you act the part you give yourself. Beliefs become habits and habits are nothing more than the results of self-hypnosis. It's vital to learn how to de-hypnotise yourself from your negative beliefs and replace them with better ones.

What's so amazing when you overcome a limiting belief is that you start asking yourself (as Richard Bandler points out), what else could you be wrong about?... That in itself opens an amazing new beginning.

Here are some of the many benefits of taking the time to quiet yourself down, meditate and visualise:

- *By focusing on what you want, not what you don't want, you send a message to yourself to raise your expectations. After all, if you are going to see yourself in situations you might as well visualise the right ones.*

- *When you quiet your mind to visualise, you improve your ability to focus. The more you visualise and the better you get at it, the better your overall focus becomes.*

- *Done wisely, it helps you relax as it's a kind of meditation and can help you reduce stress.*

- *By thinking precisely about what you want, you help set your unconscious mind to work to achieve it. This means you are working toward your goals without even knowing it.*

- *You can improve your health. You can actually visualise getting better, healing yourself. You can visualise your body rebuilding itself. Tests have shown that it makes a difference.*

- *Improve your self image. The more you see the ideal you going through all the things you need to do to achieve your aims, there is a positive effect on your mind. The result is that you become happier and more confident.*

- *When you vividly imagine achieving your goals you trigger a whole series of subconscious processes that will help you reach your target.*

6. Timelines

One of the most powerful and exciting visualisation exercises involves timelines. I highly recommend you practise timelines at least a few times a year.

Timelines are largely about visualisation. For example, if I ask you to picture what you will be doing tomorrow, you will create a mental image of what you'll be doing and it will take up a certain area in your field of vision, with an imaginary distance from you.

Now, here's the thing. When you think about something you're doing next week, it's a safe bet this new image occurs in a different part of your field of vision. You might notice your eyes refocus as you think of the new image. You might even point to a place some way off where you imagine this future event occurring. Something a month off will be in another place again.

Many people imagine their future stretches ahead of them and their past stretches away behind them. I highly recommend practising this technique with someone, ideally a timeline therapist or someone who is NLP trained.

Imagine yourself 'going into the future', say one year from now, and seeing what you have learned, what you have managed to accomplish, then do the same again, but for 5 years in the future, and then 10 years. Make sure to go in deep, visualise with precision. See what you would see, hear what you would hear and feel what you would feel. What is really amazing is what happens when you imagine getting to the end of your days and you turn round and look back, toward the present.

Looking back from your imagined future can have a powerful effect. You can see what is really important to you and you will understand the really important things in life: relationships, those great memories. . .

When you have learned so much from your future self, then come back to the present, and bring all those learnings back with you. It's an enriching experience.

This is just one of the uses of visualisation. There is another, which can powerfully and dramatically change your attitude to life—and your life in particular!

7. The Law of Attraction

The Law of Attraction is a truly powerful tool to help you get what you want. At its heart, the Law of Attraction is a belief that by focusing on positive or negative thoughts you will attract to you positive or negative experiences. Essentially, you get what you focus on.

The Law of Attraction uses visualisation of desired outcomes to replace limiting or self-destructive thinking. It combines reframing techniques with affirmations to generate a particular attitude to the world. You feel like the changes you want have already occurred. What is amazing is that time and time again, those people who start to use the Law of Attraction really do start to see very real changes in their lives, with improvements in their health, wealth and relationships.

It's a means of sending out a particular message to the universe of happiness, gratitude and optimism, and it expects the universe to reciprocate.

To find out more about the Law of Attraction, check out *The Secret*. The experts on the film explain in great detail the reasoning behind it, and how our thoughts and what we invite into our lives can help us achieve or dreams and goals.

I am a great believer in the Law of Attraction. I also believe anything and everything in life requires work and commitment. You have to put the work in and have a clear plan; you can't expect only to visualise it, or to want to attract it and it will become a reality.

8. Gratitude

Central to the Law of Attraction is the idea of fostering a powerful sense of gratitude to the universe. With such a powerful attitude to the world, you notice more of the good things around you, and you see a world filled with ever more opportunity.

It is a deeply positive experience to recognise all the things that have gone right in your life. It helps you see the world with greater optimism.

And let's face it, you do have a lot of things to be grateful for.

Here are a few:

First of all, we are all winners. We all come from a successful sperm and egg that 'joined forces' to create you.

From the very beginning of time our ancestors created families and environments based on love, loyalty, friendship, and a deep respect and admiration and love for their parents, brothers and sisters. And in the toughest times, they survived and kept your ancestors on the earth. Even through the toughest time, they survived—and that's why you're here.

What is there to complain about?

And do you complain?

Do you whine?

Are you a moaner and a cry-baby?

Be honest. If that's the case, let's make a conscious decision to move away from complaining about things.

When I am struggling, I think to myself, *could I have imagined doing what I am doing now, 10 years ago?* What would I have been willing to give up or sign up for to be where I am today?

And of course, if where I am today is not so great as it was 10 years ago—then there's a positive lesson there, too. *Things change and I've been in a better place before, and I will be again.*

In the latter case, rather than feel sorry for myself, I consider how lucky I really am. I remember there are so many who have nothing, who live in complete poverty, who are *really* underprivileged.

Let's look at what you're doing now.

Are you reading this book?

Does that mean it's safe for me to assume you have eyes and you can actually read?

Or does it mean you can listen and hear?

That's a powerful positive, already. Then there's the fact that we live in a society that allows books and reading, that has ensured you're educated.

So when you're having what you think is a 'bad day', listen to yourself.

Do you hear yourself 'whingeing'?

If so, come up with a mantra that works for you: you choose.

When you hear the negative voice, it might well be something simple, like: 'Shut up', 'Shut the fuck up', 'Stop'. . . or a softer approach could simply be to say to yourself 'SHUSH!'

Get that internal dialogue under control. Now.

Chapter 5

YOUR SPIRIT

Summary

1. Foundation and Practice

In the previous pages we've reviewed the common denominators of some successful, inspiring and influential people who have left and are leaving a positive mark on this planet.

Finding your 'Resilience' within you, welcoming your 'Revolution' and moving forward with your 'Reinvention' are basic foundations you can use to succeed in life.

Let me insist on the foundations. In a previous part of my life I used to have a construction company. Architects and builders understand the importance of finding firm soil to build a strong, solid house. You need strong foundations if you are ambitious and you want to go far in life; you will need deeper foundations with thicker iron and more concrete in order to reach the stars.

You've seen some of the necessary practices of the successful and those who bring about successful change.

Healthy Body—Healthy Mind—Healthy Spirit.

You've discovered their attitudes to the world, how they think and get in contact with their thoughts, get control of their egos and go for what they really want in life. All of the above is based on being truthful to yourself and avoiding living a lie.

There is more to explore, but I've given you the starting points—physical health, mental health, wise mindful practice and optimism.

So, master these skills. Practice, practice, practice.

Start now.

In his 2008 book *Outliers*, Malcolm Gladwell wrote about the amount of time it takes to perfect doing something — anything — estimating that 'ten thousand hours is the magic number of greatness.'

Gladwell studied numerous different elite performers, and claimed it's 'an extraordinarily consistent answer in an incredible number of fields. . . you need to have practised, to have apprenticed, for 10,000 hours before you get good.'

Gladwell wasn't saying that anyone can be a genius in 10,000 hours, but in order for someone to master a skill — really master it and realise their innate skills, then that was the time it took.

Start now, look back over the hints, attitudes and skills in this book and try to make them part of your life. Start NOW.

It's the biggest question of all:

How are you going to change, personally and professionally, right now?

---

2. Setting an Achievable Direction

If you want to improve your life—that's fantastic! I'm with you and I'm here to show you the way.

So, first things first. Let's look at what you want to change and make sure you are asking for something achievable.

When you set out on your journey of change, making sure you're asking for the right things is important, as is making sure you aren't judging yourself too harshly in the first place.

After all, no one is flawless or perfect. We are all ongoing 'projects' and, as long as we are on a continual path of learning and we are each morning a little bit better than the day before, then we are on the right track. Cut yourself some slack so that you can see the bigger picture and you don't only focus on short-term goals.

The questions you need to get you there:

• Is what I am aspiring to achievable?

• How important is it to me?

• Will it be good for me?

• Am I asking for too much? Or not enough?

Then ask yourself some more questions:

• What am I hoping to achieve with the changes I want?

• Is it all about me, or am I doing it to exclude everyone else? Because that is a short-term solution.

I know that becoming the best you can be is important. There are so many great mentors, and tens of thousands of other less well-known amazing mentors, coaches and trainers who can help you do that. They are all over the world and they are working every day in so many different ways. They do it through live events, mastermind workshops, our legacy clubs, books, videos, magazine articles, one-to-ones, podcasts, e-learning on social media and other ways, too. But if in the process of becoming the best you, you exclude thought about others, is that the healthiest way forward?

How about trying to make the world a better place at the same time as making you a better person? If you don't, then the path you're on will be a lonely one with few friends to accompany you along the way. And to be honest, it's selfish.

So all those questions I asked you before about making changes for yourself come with an extra question. Here is The Question:

* * *

Will the changes I make help create a better world?

* * *

I believe creating the best you HAS to equal a better world, making our life count, making a difference, or whatever you want to call it.

After all, which is better: the you who only thinks of achieving your own goals, or the you who achieves your own goals and helps others achieve theirs?

One is greater than the other.

I believe that those who help others and those interested in personal and professional development will be the game changers of the 21st century. Especially at this time in the history of the world, we need each other. We don't live in a bubble. And the world needs us!

Done with skill, there is a bigger goal to achieve than just helping yourself.

So, let's make your goal big. It's not only the best YOU we want. It's the best YOU-niverse, too.

Surely, that's only a little step, after all?

*   *   *

The Question: Where to start?

Answer: With you—you personally.

*   *   *

3. Your Personal True Purpose. Personally— Professionally—Globally

In the coming sections I'm going to ask you not one question, or The Question, but many questions. So, as we agreed, I'm going to need you to be completely honest with yourself, with no hiding from the truth.

All those questions come from the same place and are the children of the one big Question: *What are you here for?* Or, put it another way, *What is your true purpose in life? What will your legacy be?*

This chapter will explore your true purpose in life at a personal level. The next will ask more questions of your true purpose in your professional life and the next will ask questions of your true purpose on a global level.

Ambition is a vital thing. To think big means that even if you don't accomplish everything, you accomplish more than if you set tiny goals. That's why later we won't just talk about you and your work, but also about the bigger side of your life on a world scale.

This chapter will ask you about:

• Your health

• Your physical wellbeing to do with exercise

• Your love life

• Your relationships with family and friends

• Your dreams and goals

• Your legacy

Remember. Be honest. Take your time with these questions. Get a piece of paper and write down the answers you know are right. Because as The Law of Attraction tells us, taking the time to put things into writing is part of the process of harmonising with the universe and making real what you want to happen.

First. . .

Personally: You and Your Personal True Purpose

I want you to take some time to ask yourself some questions that require more true honesty.

The Questions:

• Who am I?

• How do people see me?

- What could be better about me?

- What do I want of myself?

- What is my purpose?

- Why or for what purpose do I live?

Answer those questions now. Think about them, take as much time as you need, then come back when you're ready.

* * *

1. Finding Your True Purpose

The definition of *purpose* in the dictionary is

1. *The reason for which something is done or created or for which something exists.*

2. *A person's sense of resolve or determination.*

Very few people instinctively know what they want to do with their lives. Some people stumble across it, others spend their lives looking for it.

So how do know or find your true purpose?

Mark Twain said, '*The two most important days in your life are the day you are born and the day you find out why.*'

Of course, the day you were born is important because it's when your unique consciousness entered the world. You won't remember, but there's no doubt it's the most important day of your life!

Finding out why you are on the Earth can take a long time. Some people seem to have a sense of direction and meaning from very early on—but for most people who reflect on their lives, and that probably includes you, it's not always the case that an answer opens up immediately. It takes time, reflecting on the things that you've done in your life and how you've reacted to them. It takes thinking about the things you are drawn to, and what feels right in your gut and in your heart. It needs you to think, too, about the things you aren't drawn to, that you want to avoid. Feel for what feels right inside of you, filtering and looking through the evidence to find out the very best version of yourself, to become that version. Think about the times you've resonated with things, that a note has been struck inside you. If it hasn't, yet, that also is possible—so keep looking—and listening.

One of my favourite quotes is from Parker Palmer when he says, *'Before I can tell my life what I want to do with it, I need to listen to my life to tell me who I am.'*

Take the time to listen. Take the time to sit in a quiet, relaxed, meditative space and lift the pressure off yourself. Let go of your ego in a more relaxed, safe space and look for the question and the answer that supply not just your conscious sense of self, but that make your whole being feel right. That is the moment when you resonate with your own truth.

Another quote from Parker Palmer is this one: *'Our deepest calling is to grow into our own authentic self-hood, whether or not it conforms to some image of who we ought to be. As we do so, we will not only find the joy that every human being seeks—we will also find our path of authentic service in the world.'*

This attitude should inform the answers to the questions to come.

Finding out Your Purpose
Listen to your life.

While you listen to your life, and consider all the amazing things that have happened to you, the bad things as well as the good, the times when you have felt out of kilter, the times you have felt absolutely right, you will notice that certain patterns make themselves apparent to you. There is a thread that is consistent throughout your past, that's consistent with your passion and skills. That is where your power and purpose lies.

This doesn't mean that everything you've done in the past should dictate what you do in the future. If that were the case, then there would never be any change. Quite the contrary: you are reading this book because you want change, you want to be *The Best You*. Instead, be aware that your past holds valuable information about what you really enjoy doing, and that is an indication of who you are. Finding ways to do more of that—of what brings you passion and purpose—that is what listening to your life will give you.

One of the proudest things I am developing and launching are our Best You Legacy Clubs where my Legacy Club directors and members meet once a month all over the world, we seek for purpose and what legacy really means, and we showcase amazing and inspiring people and ideas. I really believe it's going to be a global game changer!

Do More—Practise More

If you feel you haven't yet lived enough to know what your purpose is, then it's vital that you go out and experience more of life. Try new things—things that you would never normally consider, to see if those things hold answers to your questions.

Ask yourself now:

• What are the things I wouldn't normally consider?

• What have I wanted to do for a long time?

• What are other people involved in that maybe I want to taste and try?

Do something new. Do something you have never tried before. Put it down in your list of experiences. Take a course, take a journey, volunteer to do something worthwhile, take notice of people you normally ignore. Look for newness and crave fresh experiences. You'll be amazed how a bank of fresh experiences is something you can draw on later.

Trying and doing new things—really living life—will help you find your true purpose.

Teachings and Learnings

The truth is, you may not be able to realise your life purpose by yourself.

You never know what book, talk, interview or event might put you onto your true path. Find a mentor, ask those who inspire you. . . seek and you will find.

Follow your heart by seeking answers—finding teachers who have really got something to say, and then taking the time to integrate those learnings into yourself. Does what you've learned feel right? Does it speak to the authentic you?

The key is finding where your abilities and personal drive intersect the needs of others. When you help others, then you often find a sense of connection, of larger purpose than simply *making money*, or *being successful* in some vague way. The good feeling you generate in the world through being who you are, that is often the indicator you are on the right path.

In strict terms, as the Buddha noted, what you do is not who you are. If you are an author, speaker, thinker, mentor, those are the ways that your passion is expressed. Your true purpose lies deeper down than the job titles you give yourself.

I believe there isn't only one purpose. When you embrace life fully, when you get off the sofa and are open to learning, ready to explore, ready to be pushed, when you live a passionate life, that is where some of your answers lie. In some ways, by engaging and acting in a wise and kind way with the rest of the world, what you do becomes the expression of your purpose.

The Questions you need to ask yourself:

What would I do and who would I be if money didn't hold me back?

What do I love?

What am I good at?

And most importantly. . .

What injustices are out there that really bug me or annoy me?

What does the world need and how can I help?

2. The Tough Questions

The Inventory Check of the Soul

Let's do an inventory check of who you are and what you are. Let's find out what you represent, what your values are, what you are proud of, who and what you love and what you like to do.

Before we do, it's worth taking a moment to find the things that are right in your life. To send out to the universe a wave of gratitude. By doing so, you'll begin to see the extraordinary good fortune you enjoy.

Things to be grateful for—ask yourself:

What am I assuming or taking for granted?

It may sound obvious, and I have said it before—but if you can see, can stand, and have your limbs then you have plenty to be grateful for. And if not, then you are still here, and able to read and hear this book and others. You are safe. Hopefully, no wars are about to sweep over you. You live in civilisation. These are all things to be grateful for.

You have managed to use some kind of method of transport to be where you are. Maybe you have a phone or some form or way of communicating with others? Do you have a home? Electricity? Running water? Can I assume you have something to eat tonight, maybe tomorrow?

These are small things, but there are many who do not have them.

*   *   *   *

285 million people are estimated to be visually impaired worldwide.

39 million are blind.

90 per cent of the world's visually impaired live in low-income settings.

Over 5 per cent of the world's population—360 million people—has disabling hearing loss (328 million adults and 32 million children).

1.3 billion people live without electric lighting. (More than 600 million of them are in sub-Saharan Africa and more than 300 million are in India alone).

2.4 billion people still lack improved sanitation.

946 million people do not have toilets.

663 million people live without access to safe water.

More than 1 million annual limb amputations occur globally—one every 30 seconds.

285 million people suffer from diabetes, a figure expected to reach 435 million by 2030.

More than 6 per cent of the population aged 20–79 years in EU countries, or 33 million people, have diabetes.

*   *   *

So, are you feeling luckier now?

It's time to compile that inventory of your life.

Sit down and make a list of as many things as you can think of that really resonate truthfully for you in each box. Remember don't let the ego get in the way:

What do I like about me?	What do I love about my life?	What am I grateful for?	What do I want to change?	What would l love to do?

What are you here for? The Questions to ask yourself:

1. Are you here to become as unhappy as possible?

   OR Are you here to become as happy as you can be?

   Ask yourself:

   How can I become happier?

2. Are you here to eat and drink as much as you can and not take care of yourself?

   OR Are you here to eat healthily and live as long as you can?

   Ask yourself:

   How can I eat healthily and live as long as possible?

3. Are you here to live without caring about your kids?

    OR Do you want a great relationship with your kids here so they love you and look up to you?

    Ask yourself:

    How can I make my kids look up to me, respect me, love me?

4. Are you here to cheat on your wife or your husband?

    OR Are you here to love your spouse with all your heart?

    Ask yourself:

    How can I show my partner I love them with all my heart?

5. Are you here to be a selfish lover?

    OR Are you here to become the best lover your partner has ever had?

    Ask yourself:

    How can I become the best lover my partner has ever had?

6. Are you here to be sad and make other people's lives miserable?

    OR Are you here to make other people's lives better and make yourself and everyone happier?

    Ask yourself:

    How can I make other people happier around me?

7. Are you here to be negative and hold yourself back?

    OR Are you here to be a positive person and make a difference in this world?

    Ask yourself:

    How can I make a difference in the world?

8. Are you here to see your life go by?

    OR Are you here to live a fulfilling life?

    Ask yourself:

    How can I live my most fulfilling life?

3. Your World

Your Health—Your Physical Fitness

Take a moment to consider your body.

How do you feel?

Are you slow and sluggish?

Does your body feel too heavy?

Do you feel like you haven't got a good body shape?

Do you feel your fitness stops you from doing things?

How would you like to feel? How would you like to look?

The skill with having the right weight is ensuring that you balance the right sort of food with exercise. This keeps you in the weight zone you want.

When you are younger, your calories burn quicker, but it is scary to see how many people are literally 'Killing themselves slowly' by steady overeating—and at the same time killing their kids slowly, too.

Is your weight something you've ignored for too long?

Be honest. If you know you are eating too much and that prevents you from feeling well, if it makes you feel bad about yourself, well, you know you need to do something.

If that is the case, what stops you?

How do you overcome what stops you?

For your own sake and for your own future, be honest. Don't give yourself excuses.

A change in your eating habits is going to feel strange at first—and for some people that is a thing to fear. You shouldn't fear being what you think is uncomfortable, it is only unfamiliar.

And be honest, what is the alternative?

You've recognised there's something wrong, that you don't feel well, so how do you think you will change? By doing the same thing or doing something different with your exercise and food?

Welcome being 'uncomfortable'. Welcome the unfamiliar. Break your usual habits and routines!

As the popular saying goes:

> *'Insanity is doing the same thing over and over again and expecting different results.'*

* * *

English dietary expert Jason Vale is known as the Juice Master. His mission is to get everyone eating more healthily and to get a juicer in everyone's home.

Jason observes that people in Britain complain about the British health service, the NHS, saying that it is overstretched, that there are fewer services and so on.

At the same time, he notes that people are more obese than ever. The NHS is having to do amputations due to diabetes, perform stomach reductions, operate for heart conditions due to poor diets and lack of exercise, and deal with lung conditions due to heavy smoking.

He asks the question: if people are really concerned about the NHS, then why are they living lifestyles that put so much strain on it? If you want a good health service, he says then 'Don't ask what can the NHS do for you but what can you do for the NHS.'

Too often, people expect others to take responsibility for our faults and failures as human beings.

But what is responsibility?

It means to be answerable for actions or a situation. Why, then, should a health service answer for your actions?

Think about responsibility in another way. Think about it as being able to respond. Think of it as your power to do something useful. No one else's.

You are responsible for your fitness. So—respond!

*   *   *

We reviewed your physical fitness at more length in a previous chapter. The fact is the more exercise you do the better you will feel. Find something you like to do—whether it's walking, swimming, dancing, cycling, yoga. Try new things. Make it work for you. And make your body work for you, too

Value yourself. Give yourself 'me time'. Even 20 minutes of exercise a day is better than none. A half hour is better than 20 minutes, and an hour better than a half.

Get hooked on something that's good for you. As well as exercise, take time to meditate, to have a healthy lunch, to read.

Give yourself the time to think, to grow new habits—and to change!

* * * *

What are you here for?

The Questions to ask yourself:

1. Would you like to be unhealthy?

    OR Would you like to be healthy?

    Ask yourself:

    How can I become healthier?

2. Are you looking to die young?

    OR Would you like to live longer?

    Ask yourself:

    How can I live longer?

3. Would you like to teach your kids how to eat the wrong things?

    OR Would you like to teach your kids how to eat healthily?

    Ask yourself:

    What can I do to help them to eat healthier?

4. Would you prefer watching TV and ignoring your health?

OR would you prefer to exercise and feeling good about yourself?

Ask yourself:

What exercise am I doing today?

Use your answers as the starting point of making real changes in your life.

Your Family—What Do You Want?

Relationships can be complicated. Family is family—and as the old saying goes, you can't choose them. You may have been brought up in a beautiful loving home, loved and adored. Maybe the relationships you have with your siblings mean that they are your best friends. If so, that is amazing.

'*The quality of your life is the quality of your relationships.*'

—Tony Robbins

Your Parents

On the other hand, maybe a parent or both parents weren't a great example. Maybe they were abusive or absent.

If your relationship with your parents wasn't great, has it affected you to a point where you are not being the best parent you could be?

If so, The Question has to be:

What can you learn from how you were brought up?

How can you become a better parent than your own were to you?

On the other hand, if you are still lucky enough to have them around, are you good friends?

How good? Do you talk with them often? Is there something you need to tell them?

Is there something you need to say to clear the air?

Do you need to forgive so that you can get back on track?

But if your relationship with them is not great, please understand that you are not going to change them, stop trying to and remember that you choose how you feel.

Or is it simpler than that?

Do you need to speak with them and give them a straightforward 'I love you'?

If so, there is never *a* perfect time to do that. It's *always* the perfect time!

Don't miss out. Life's too short to leave things unsaid. Put what you feel in writing if it makes it easier. Be old-fashioned. Send a letter today to your parent or parents and tell them how much you appreciate what they have done and continue to do.

Siblings
Let's talk about your relationship with your brothers and sisters.

What is that like?

Do you speak often?

Have you given up on a loved one?

Does a sibling need your help?

Relationships with brothers and sisters can be difficult. I think about my own experience. I was part of a very large Spanish family, and all my father's brothers and their families used to get together with my grandparents every weekend. Those weekends were happy times. There were loads of cousins playing and laughing, lots of eating and fun. Of course, I have fond memories of those times. My father was the eldest, and I remember he always used to love bringing all the family together to go out and eat, or come to large gatherings at my house. My father loved this, and so did the rest of the family. It's something I learned from him and my mum, and it's something I like to continue in my own life.

If you have a brother and sister and they have kids, remember they are blood. Spoil them, love them, let them know you are there for them. Make sure you are. Whatever you do make sure at the end of your life you have no regrets, just because you haven't said the things you should have said or done what you should have done.

Do you have kids of your own?

Be honest with yourself. What could you do better?

Do you take as many chances as possible to play with them or educate them?

Are you teaching them the right values?

Do you love them as much as you can and should?

Do you squeeze and cuddle them at every chance you have?

Remember, they grow up very quickly and there will come a day when it's not cool to do that. Promising yourself you'll spend time with them and not doing so is making a date with regret!

So, do you spend too much time watching TV or on the computer or phone instead of appreciating how magical and amazing they are?

If they are now older and have moved away, how can you connect, create a better bond? How can you support them?

Do you have any regrets?

Does your child or children need to know how much you care?

Have you told them how amazing they are and how much you love them?

Or how proud you are of them?

What are you here for? The Questions to ask yourself:

1. Would you like to be a bad son or daughter to your parents?

   OR Would you like to be a loving and caring one?

   Ask yourself:

   How can I become the best son or daughter I can be?

2. Are you on this planet to be a terrible brother or sister?

   OR would you like to be the best brother or sister ever?

   Ask yourself:

   How can I become a better sibling? What do I need to do?

Your Love Life

First of all let's look at the definition of love: a strong feeling of affection, great interest and pleasure in something, to feel deep affection or sexual love for (someone). *Or the definition of loving:* a profoundly tender, passionate affection for another person. A feeling of warm personal attachment or deep affection, as for a parent, child, or friend. Sexual passion or desire. A person toward whom love is felt; beloved person; sweetheart.

There is nothing like being in love; there is nothing like loving someone, kissing passionately, and thinking about them as you do all day, every hour. . .when you simply can't get them out of your mind, or those beautiful 'butterfly' feelings you get when you stand next to them.

Being IN LOVE is such a beautiful place to be.

This is a quote from my friend Luca Martinelli:

He declared with that force of certainly and authority he owns so powerfully, that a woman should only ever give herself to a man who adores her, who looks at her with a passion that burns, who cannot help but to touch her skin when near her, even if just in an apologetic accidental graze of her hand—as he subtly touched the back of my hand in demonstration. How a man should be so taken by a woman he struggles to find his words when he first sees her. He could have been explaining how he expected if not demanded a man to treat his daughter. There is no doubt this is what he would hope for his daughter. I adore this about him.

Are you married or single? If you're single, are you happy flitting from date to date? Are you at that stage where you are happy-go-lucky and have no commitments and no ties? Or are you ready to settle down?

Remember, once you've decided to go all in it's never about 'me' first. it's about 'us' or 'my partner' first and 'me' last.

Plan ahead a little. Flitting from relationship to relationship can be fun, but remember, the older you get, the harder it becomes to let someone really share your life.

Are you looking for love?

Do you want a family?

If you are planning one, are you really prepared to commit?

I am very proud of my children and I often say they are my real legacy to the world. Could I or should I have been a better parent? Yes, of course, but still too many people nowadays get into marriage simply to divorce after a few years—it seems people aren't really prepared to put the work in. A marriage is sometimes not easy but ideally kids need both parents to grow more balanced. I am not saying that it has to be the case. After all, many times marriages are unhealthy and unhappy. Are you prepared to make things work?

Remember the timeline exercise in which you go into your future?

Try different futures out. Ones where you get to later life with a partner, and one without.

What do you feel about one day finding yourself alone without a long-term partner and without kids?

How does that feel?

Think. What do you want in an ideal world?

What are you here for?

The Questions to ask yourself:

1. When you get to the end of your life, do you want to be surrounded by a family that loves you?

   OR Do you want to be alone?

   Ask yourself:

   How can you find value and meaning in your friendships and relationships through to your dying days?

2. Do you want to enjoy a really close relationship with someone over the long term?

   OR Are you happy to stay on the surface with no ties and commitments?

Ask yourself:

Are you ready for something more? Do you think you will be one day?

3.   Do you think you would make a good parent?

OR Are you not ready yet—but one day, do you think you will be?

Ask yourself:

What are the different rewards in life from different family scenarios? Which is better for you?

Marriage

Let's talk about marriage and cohabitation.

Perhaps you are already married or in a long-term relationship where you live together. If so, do you appreciate your relationship? If you're unmarried, do you hope to get married one day?

It has often been said that the family is the basic building block of our society. Every marriage requires hard work and commitment from both parties to succeed. It needs you to get together, to look at the long-term plan and continuously work on it. It requires you to keep communicating, sharing, loving, keeping the flame alive all the time you are together. It isn't just a happy wedding day. It is a life shared at the deepest level.

Our grandparents married for life: 'till death do us part' meant exactly that. Now, things have changed and divorce rates have grown rapidly.

I have been married for 32 years and we were definitely the exception to the current norm of marriages not lasting that long.

My very basic advice to you is to keep working at it. Life will throw things at you, but it's how you deal with those challenges that tests your commitment, not only to marriage but also to yourself and to your life. Treasuring those beautiful moments with your spouse and your kids is a defence against disappointment and disenchantment. Those moments are like magic. What I have is an amazing collection of beautiful memories, which can only fill me with joy. Gathering more such memories, that too is part of the personal purpose of my life.

Get down to basics. However you divide up the work you do in your home life, and the tasks each of you has, it can be done with care and kindness or with a toughness. Which is better?

The Questions to ask yourself:

1. Do you compliment your partner and show them love and treasure them?

    OR Do you simply take them for granted, even though you treasure them on the inside?

    Ask yourself:

    What are you going to do to make them know how much you care?

2. Do you do things for you partner? Do you shop for them? Cook for them? Hold their hand? Stroke their hair? Bring a smile to their face when they are down. Do you show the love? Do you kiss? Do you massage each other? Are you physical enough?

Or do you remain unexpressive and keep your feelings hidden?

Ask yourself:

How do you physically and emotionally show the love?

The Call of Affairs

Have you had an affair in the past, are you playing around or are you looking to play around?

In some countries, having an affair is more accepted by society than others.

The French are famed for having a more liberal attitude towards fidelity and sex. They also have a name for the affair that occurs between a person leaving the office and getting home. They call it a *cinq à sept*—literally, a five till seven, which gives a couple of hours to squeeze in a sexual escapade.

In Anglo Saxon culture, infidelity rates haven't changed much over the decades. Research estimates that nearly 60 per cent of men and more than 45 per cent of women are unfaithful at some point. More than one-third of couples are affected by affairs.

How do affairs happen? The temptations are too varied and numerous to list. Working closely with someone is a common cause, in which closeness becomes something more.

On the other side, a sense of neglect from a preoccupied partner, the sense of being in a rut, of wanting to bring excitement to your life—these can all be factors. Then there's the classic mid-life crisis. That old question: do I still have what it takes to attract someone else? As if you have to prove something to yourself.

There is no single way to run a marriage. Some people manage to have affairs and keep their marriage alive, some couples agree that they will keep their relationship special but will also sleep with others. But vital to such an approach is honest communication—finding out what the limits are for you and your partner, and even if it can happen without derailing your marriage.

Talking openly is the key.

Remember, too, that having an affair is one of the most hurtful things you can do to someone. It strikes at the foundation of their trust in you. Discussing what you each want from your ideal marriage will put your potential future into perspective and reveal the possibilities open to you.

I am not endorsing or recommending an affair; far from it. Maybe you believe in an open marriage and it might work for you. It is simply a fact of life that some couples find a way to accommodate that approach to marriage. At its heart is the question of what you and your partner want from your marriage.

Can you forgive the other?

Can they forgive you?

Would you stay with them after this?

Ask yourself:

Am I prepared for the consequences of my actions?

Am I prepared for the pain I am going to inflict on my spouse (and kids)?

Is it best to be honest or to lie?

What is the best thing to do?

If I am not happy, what is the best way to move on?

There are no right and wrong answers to these questions. But if this is where you are in life, then you will need to think carefully about the answers. Seek help and guidance from trusted friends or a professional. It is not easy, but only by examining your actions and asking yourself these questions can you hope to move forward.

What are you here for? The Questions to ask yourself:

Have I already moved on in my mind?

Am I more interested in the affair than living at home?

Do I care about this marriage?

Do I want to spend the rest of my life with him/her?

Do I want to stay married?

Am I prepared to work hard at it?

Ask yourself: What would be best for both of us?

Are you questioning the future of your marriage?

Often, commencing an affair is part of a recognition that your marriage is coming to an end. That there are things you cannot get inside marriage that you are no longer willing to sacrifice your happiness for.

Are you asking yourself questions? Are you happy? Is it one of the easiest or most difficult decisions you have ever made or are about to make?

Are you going through what others may call a 'mid-life crisis' or what I call transition, or simply questioning things?

There is a story about a man seeking a diamond mine that will make him rich beyond his wildest dreams. He travels the world for years, seeking it, seeking the riches that will make him truly happy, and never finds it. Eventually, he returns back home, unsuccessful, only to find that his house sits on a massive lode of diamonds. . .

Sometimes, then, happiness and fulfilment are staring us in the face, but we don't have the eyes to look. Our happiness and contentment lies within us.

There is no definitive right answer to these questions. It's not a test that will score you points at an exam. Each decision you make will have its outcomes, and it's up to you to ask the right questions to make the best decision for you—and everyone else around you.

What are you here for? Ask yourself

The questions:

Is my spouse supportive?

Does he/she believe in me?

Is he/she my friend?

Do I adore him/her?

Do I want to spend the rest of my life with him/her?

Would you like to live in an unhappy marriage?

OR Would you like to be happy in your marriage?

So ask yourself:

How or what can I do to keep our marriage alive?

What made me fall in love with him/her in the first place?

What do I adore about him/her?

Does the fact of being free attract me more than being with him/her?

Is it worth fighting for?

How can I make this work?

Are you divorced?

In the last few years, divorce has dropped to its lowest rate in 40 years, perhaps as a result of increased cohabitation before marriage. An estimated 42 per cent of marriages in the UK currently end in divorce, but figures among lower age groups are starting to show a marked decline.

Knowing what it's like to live with someone and making it work before marriage seems to have strengthened the institution of marriage.

At the same time, the rate of divorce for older couples is at its highest ever.

So where are you in life?

Have you been married and got divorced?

Are you over that now?

Are you enjoying the single life?

Are you actually looking for love or simply having fun and enjoying life?

So, are you able to do the things you wanted to do, now that you have no one to answer to?

Maybe you have small children and your duties are pretty much the same, but the question is, are you making as much as possible of your life?

What's stopping you?

When we are younger, we have dreams for our future, but as we get older we get caught in 'the system' and tend to forget who we really wanted to be or what we really wanted to do in our lives. Being single now is an opportunity to start finding the true you. Now's the time to really explore and think about what your next chapter really is.

The Questions:

First of all, do you regret divorcing?

Are you really looking for a new relationship?

Is there anything else you would like to do before?

For those seeking for love, are you trying too hard?

Do you think it's too late for you?

Are you unrealistic with your expectations?

Are you looking for the 'perfect' man or woman?

Do you think you have lost your mojo?

A very inspiring woman I interviewed for *The Best You* magazine was Roz Savage, MBE, who holds four Guinness World Records for ocean rowing, including being the first woman to row solo across the Atlantic, Pacific and Indian Ocean. Roz had been a keen rower at Oxford University, but then went on to spend 11 years as a management consultant.

One day, Roz was travelling on a train and wrote two versions of her own obituary—one where she carried on living as she was then, the other following her heart's desire (remember the timeline exercise? This is a similar idea.) The difference between what she could be and what she was then spurred her to leave her old life behind and start anew. She divorced, and became a keen environmentalist and activist, a member of the Royal Geographic Society who is making a real impact on the world through her environmental work.

It's an amazing and heartening story.

What is your adventure?

What do you want to become?

Who will you be now that you have the choices you never had before?

What or who is stopping you?

If you are looking for new love, then give yourself a chance to find it. I am a great believer that those who are confident in their own skin, congruent with their thoughts and actions, radiate confidence.

Tall, short, small, thin, chubby, happy, grumpy, young, old—people have and will always find love. I also think people often look too hard and don't let love happen. They work too hard. Love is spontaneous—you simply never know when you will find true love.

What are you here for? Ask yourself

The questions:

Should you focus on your adventure, or on finding love?

How open are you to love?

How confident are you that you will find it?

Are you realistic in your expectations?

Do you want to spend the rest of your life with the person you are seeing now?

* * *

Whatever your case may be, here's a quote that I adore:

"Tis better to have loved and lost than never to have loved at all.'

—Alfred Lord Tennyson

* * *

Friends

What does friendship mean to you?

The definition in the dictionary: *a person with whom one has a bond of mutual affection, typically one exclusive of sexual or family relations.*

Are you still friends with some people you grew up with? How often do you speak? I still have some friends from my youth. It's true I don't speak with them or see them as much as I would like. Will I regret it? Probably! Which means it's time I did something about it. And you?

The idea of keeping your friends from your youth may be a great idea, but the fact is that with age one becomes less patient—it's safe to say! I think the reason I lost a lot of friends over the years is that we probably started seeing things differently. Our perspective in life changed, we had different priorities and values. Then we had our own families and simply grew apart.

We all probably have some friends that still live as if they were in their teens, 20 years later. You may have friends who fit into easy labels—the joker, the dramatic one, the negative one—but hopefully you also have the one you have a laugh with, the one who is your rock.

The thing is, we get so involved in our daily life and routines that friends tend to be the last on our lists. Maybe they should be at the top.

On the other hand, you should not fear getting rid of someone who drags you down with negative comments aimed at you, your dreams or plans. Your life will be so much better without that negative energy.

The Questions to ask yourself:

>Do you work at your friendship?
>
>Do you put the time in?
>
>Are you one of those who takes the calls but never rings?
>
>Do you have supportive friends?
>
>Do some of them believe in you no matter what?
>
>Are you a good friend, a true friend?
>
>Do you invest time in your friends?
>
>Have you told them recently how you feel about them?
>
>Are you still friends with people who have a negative effect on you?

More Questions to ask yourself:

>How can I become a better friend?
>
>What do I need my friends to do for me?
>
>What have I not been doing as a friend lately?
>
>What are my dreams and goals?
>
>What is my legacy?
>
>What am I here for?

Professional Life

This section is designed to explore your true purpose in your professional life. And it's absolutely vital that you get this right. Of course, your home life and the relationships you enjoy within it are central to your life—but for most people, their professional life adds a whole new layer of purpose and meaning to their time on Earth. Of course, at the same time, it provides the basics for a living. But a truly authentic engagement with your career, your work, your profession—a passionate pursuit of your purpose through work rather than simply pulling in enough money to eat and have shelter—is vital to making your life more than simply walking a treadmill.

In this section I want you to explore your ambitions, the things you want from life in the world of work.

Your Purpose in Life Professionally

When you discover your true authentic self, that realisation harnesses your passions and your energies to help you become a more authentic person in other areas of your life. Your work, your profession, is an expression of who you are. By tuning in your work with your values and true attitudes, you will find more energy for your work, enjoy it more and achieve more. Indeed, when that happens, it stops becoming work.

An old saying I am sure you have heard attributed to Chinese philosopher Confucius says: '*Choose a job you love, and you will never have to work a day in your life.*'

The Questions to ask yourself:

What do I hate about my current job role or career?

What am I doing to do something differently?

Why don't I do something else?

What does a bad day look like?

What is it I don't enjoy about my job and why?

What does failure look like beyond my pay cheque?

What does real failure feel like for me?

What should I try and avoid?

Why do I do what I do?

What thrills me about my current job role or career, if any?

What does a great day look like?

What does success look like beyond my pay cheque?

What does real success feel like for me?

How do I want to feel about the impact on the world when I retire?

I believe many people pursue a career they are not necessarily interested in. They spend their lives working in something they are not engaged by or passionate about. That's fine as far as it goes. I get that not everyone can have the job of their dreams. For many people it's a balancing act. Their passion is something they don't believe they can pursue. They feel a duty to their commitments and so follow their passion in their spare time: a hobby that they throw themselves into—that also can be a wonderful life-enhancing thing to do.

For many, though, it's just that they haven't yet seen a way to make their passion pay its way. It's a question of self-belief, and learning to believe in the possibilities life presents, identifying those opportunities around you and going for it.

That might mean learning new things—filling in the gaps in your knowledge to give you the power to act. The fact that you have a job, a family or very little money does not stop you learning. Pursue your passions. Whatever rocks you or creates a fire in your belly—that is what you should concentrate your energies on!

1. Student

You will need to do research. Not just research for your studies, but research about what it is you really want to do. You'll need to put the years in and then, depending on what your career is, hope that you are able to use your career to take you to the place you really want to be and get the life you really want to have. On the way, you may need to change—truths will strike you as your life unfolds about who you really are and about the passion you want to pursue. That means you should be prepared to change your career, if necessary, and make sure that throughout your life you carry on reading and learning so you are constantly improving and changing. Listen to your gut, and follow the voice within.

Twenty years ago, the idea of a professional game player—that is, someone making a living from having others watch them play video games—was the stuff of science fiction. The idea of a YouTube millionaire was unheard of and social media tycoons were not even guessed at. There were no rules to adhere to in order to get those jobs, no career paths to follow. Those jobs came from the new opportunities that opened as technology advanced.

The same is happening now. And what's more, old jobs are going to disappear at a faster and faster rate.

Artificial intelligence is coming, and the reality is that technology will take over so many of what we consider everyday jobs today. In the near future, the following jobs are going to disappear:

Supermarket cashiers

Postal workers

Taxi drivers as we know them now

Lorry drivers

Food delivery workers

. . . all sorts of gig economy jobs will be automated.

Then there are the other jobs that are already threatened. . .

Travel agents

Insurance salespeople

Insurance assessors

Loss adjusters

Logistics advisers

Accountancy firms

. . . in fact, countless forms of middle management positions are right now having algorithms worked out that will see those roles reduced or automated.

Right now, they're programming computers to write books and songs. There's going to be a massive workforce that's no longer got work. We're going to see huge dislocations in work.

It also means there are going to be countless new opportunities. It's your job and my job to be ready for the change, for the next revolution, and find and take the chances we need to succeed. It might well be that the real job you want to do and that will bring you true happiness doesn't exist. . . yet.

But the world is changing at a faster and faster pace and you have to learn to adapt quickly.

That's why, if you work for a living, you should never give up on finding your dream job, never give up on learning something new, on becoming an entrepreneur and on doing something fulfilling. The time will soon be right for you to shine.

2. Working for Others

Finding your dream job is, in many cases, not an immediate option for most people. After all, you have to pay the bills and working for someone else may be the way to go, if that's the stage in life you're at, or that's where you see your path. But working for a company that cares about its employees, the environment and the world's issues is also important. Nearly everyone started at some point working for someone; the employed workforce in the West represents around half the population.

If you work in an organisation, make your contribution count. Remember about being the best you can be? That also means contributing to being part of a better world. You can do that in work. Be part of the solution. Influence policy if that's the level you're at. If lower down, share books, ideas and talks that can help you and your colleagues. Encourage a positive workplace and an environment that respects equal rights. The more people are succeeding, the better the world is going to be, so there is no point holding others back with negative thinking. Find the positive energy in your workplace.

That might also include an ethical stance, not only to others but also to the wider world. I said we all have a responsibility to be in the world. So, recycling, avoiding the use of plastic, raising funds or creating awareness of great causes is something you can be part of. If it's not happening, encourage it to happen.

Remember, The Best You + The Best Environment + The Best Place to Work = A Better World

That's a formula worth remembering.

3. Entrepreneurship

I'm a massive fan of entrepreneurship and I encourage everyone to explore the rewards and freedom it brings. It is said that entrepreneurs are a strange breed, the only people who are willing to work double the hours for half the pay and even no pay.

For those who want to be an entrepreneur, it's about finding that amazing, great idea that will make money, and pursuing it with a passion. Have you got what it takes to come up with an idea or a concept that can revolutionise. . .

anything? Anything that can make people's lives easier? Then that is something to explore, dedicate yourself to and follow up.

Question—is that entrepreneurial spirit better directed working *for* people?

Does entrepreneurship come from a better place when the entrepreneur cares about you, your needs and the world's needs? I'd suggest it does.

The world is packed full of amazing success stories from people who had a great idea and the drive to do it. There are so many businesses that started at home or literally in a garage, with one or two employees, that are now global brands.

If there is any particular denominator with all successful people, it is vision and action. One of Tony Robbins' best-known quotes is '*The path to success is to take massive determined action*'.

Amazon, Apple, Disney, Harley Davidson, Hewlett Packard, Lotus Cars and Mattel are just a few success stories. A personal favourite of mine is the story that of Subway.

Fred DeLuca founded Subway in 1965 using $1000 from his friend and later business partner, Peter Buck. Their original plan was to open 32 stores over a 10-year period. However, after nine years, they realised they weren't going to meet their goal, so they changed their business model and started franchising. That was the answer they needed.

Few people realise that Subway now has more outlets throughout the world than McDonald's. Subway has more than 34,000 locations in 98 countries, and has a turnover in the tens of billions of dollars. What's more, it's still privately owned, by DeLuca and Buck's company Doctor's Associates.

There are some obvious points I should say about entre-preneurship. Going into business is not always going to be rosy. It's tough to take that responsibility on yourself, and it requires a shift in mindset and expectation. So many people fear failure, not realising that what they think of as 'failure' is simply part of the process of growing and learn-ing. To be frank, many of the best entrepreneurs have failed many times, been rejected and ignored. So, have no fear of failure. Be brave and be prepared to press on and go against the odds.

Many, many business people have failed before finally tast-ing success:

• Bill Gates started a business called Traf-O-Data before he founded Microsoft. It went nowhere. What's more, Gates also dropped out of Harvard.

• Soichiro Honda was turned down after applying for his first job as an engineer. That's when he decided to start making scooters under his own brand. Safe to say, things went well for him!

• Thomas Edison was in the unfortunate position of being the schoolboy whose teacher told him he was too stu-pid to learn anything. That, it's fair to say, was a wrong appraisal. One of his many inventions was the lightbulb. That, too was a failure many, many times before he got a working, reliable bulb.

194 / THE QUESTION

- Walt Disney was told he 'lacked imagination and original ideas' in his first job as an editor, and was promptly fired. He opened his own animation company, which went bankrupt. He was rejected hundreds of times by investors when he sought funding to grow his business. Yet he persisted and won.

- Henry Ford was the creator of the Model T Ford, which became the iconic mass-produced car in the early 1900s. What is less well known is that his first two car companies failed, leaving him broke. He pursued his dream, however.

- Colonel Sanders was 65 years old when he founded KFC. His famous secret recipe was rejected over 1000 times before he found success.

When you're an entrepreneur, flexibility is central to your skill set. In the early days, you have to be prepared to do any job the company needs. One day you might be negotiating as CEO, another you might be washing up or cleaning the office, sweeping the floors, other days you're selling products. The spirit of entrepreneurialism is underpinned with preparedness to do whatever it takes to succeed!

Running a business is like looking after an unruly kid who permanently needs watching. When you think everything is OK and running on its own. . . boom. . . they're flat on the floor and a mess of tears! It's like that. Suddenly, you're back to square one. Monitor and monitor everything you do, and be ready to jump in quickly.

Be sure, too, that you are very aware of what you are spending money on, and how you are spending it.

My very simple advice for entrepreneurs who are setting out is to make sure you:

- Have a compelling vision of your brand. Think Big.

- Have a clear mission statement.

- Work with a great financial expert who can monitor your expenses and make sure you are going to achieve your forecast and stick to the plan!

- Understand all aspects of your business.

- Understand who your client is, your avatar.

- Understand and take care of your customers— worship them!

- Surround yourself with real experts.

- . . . And the most important one: build an amazing team and take care of them.

Let's look at some of those in more detail:

Vision

Nikola Tesla (1856–1943) was, quite literally, a visionary creator and inventor. His work included the creation of an early alternating current electricity supply system, and his achievements included the Tesla coil and early wireless-controlled boat. Tesla's strategy for creation is recorded as being one of visualisation. He was said to have such a finely tuned visual imagination that he would build his creations in his mind with precise detail before putting pen to paper, and that he could even 'test' them by visualising changing the variables while he imagined them running.

Anyone and everyone who has created, built or invented anything, visualised it in their mind first.

As an entrepreneur, it is your job to visualise your idea or company. Run it in your mind, go through all the challenges you will face, the easy and difficult decisions you will have to make, what kind of staff you should have, who your customers will be, and what they look like. Do it frequently, again and again.

If you know how to do it for yourself, visualise your timeline and look in-depth at it unfolding before you. If you're not used to working with timelines, get an NLP master practitioner, trainer or experienced guide to help you with it. Train up your unconscious so it is honed to find the opportunities that will take you on your path, so that it leads you where you see yourself going.

When it comes to having a vision, don't be shy. THINK BIG! After all, failing to do something great might mean you get something less great and a stepping stone to the thing you want. Failing to do something ordinary does not move you on at all.

Remember resilience? Failure isn't the endpoint. It's feedback. Any decent entrepreneur knows the world is packed full of stories of amazing business comebacks.

One of the books that has impacted me most in the last few years is Simon Sinek's *Start With The Why*. It's a fascinating book. What it covers are the basic aspects of companies, the ascent and descent of major global brands. There are amazing stories of how companies lost their ethos and customers turned their backs on them. There are stories of how large companies reinvented themselves and how some became the sought-after employers that so many want to work for in the world—companies like Apple, Google, Microsoft, Facebook. . .

Sinek's book and message is compelling because it's also easy and clear, and applies to everyone. He argues that if you want to inspire others, you don't start with telling them what you are going to do or how you are going to do it. These do not enthuse and motivate. As his book title says, you start with the why, set a question that needs to be answered, identify a need that needs to be met first of all. Leaders throughout history use the same technique, communicating their vision by working from the emotional engagement of 'why' before the practicalities of how and what.

To summarise:

1. The *why* comes first when you seek to inspire others.

2. Your business will thrive if your workers are emotionally engaged and excited.

3. You don't need 'dirty sales tricks' if you first demonstrate why your product is so good.

Step 1: The *why* comes first when you seek to inspire others.

The reality is that most people buy from a feeling. The what and how questions about the product you sell (i.e. what they are and how they are conceived) are secondary to that great big *why*. The why is the question that engages curiosity, that gets people interested, that makes them see things in a new light. And emotions are what you want to foster, because they then lead to buying decisions. Reason, on the other hand, often comes with adjectives attached to it like 'cold' and 'hard' because it is not about the real motivating process, which comes from passion.

When people make decisions based on strong emotions, on answering the *why* they are more engaged with it. They feel they are part of the decision-making in a more personal way. It's theirs. It belongs to them.

The *why*—that bigger vision—will encourage loyalty to an idea or a cause. Companies and successful leaders seem to offer the *why* naturally—almost effortlessly. And they're successful because people attach to it so strongly.

Think about a company like Apple and how they engage curiosity and interest by first identifying a problem that needs to be solved—they want to make a real difference in a marketplace that isn't as great as it could be. Second, they reveal the *how* of answering that. They're going to create better products that incorporate great design and a user-friendly ethos. Thirdly, they finally show us *what* their products are—computers, smart watches, telephones, tablets—and so on.

The escalation of interest from the tension of curiosity to the release through describing the *how* and the *what* means customers are ready to buy.

If you are a leader, a manager, an entrepreneur, that also should be your strategy for motivating people.

Step 2: Your business will thrive if your workers are emotionally engaged and excited.

Businesses thrive because employees are committed to them emotionally. It's not all about getting the best salary or perks. These are things that sweeten an employee's experience with a company, but they are not the core reason for someone to come on board.

If you find employees who share your vision, who care about the *why* in the same way you do, then you will have a dedicated workforce who are keen to do more for you. They'll be proactive, engaged and interested because they are inspired by your *why*.

Hire people who buy into your vision and share your why.

Step 3: You don't need 'dirty sales tricks' if you first demonstrate why your product is so good.

The key to successful customer engagement is, once again, good feelings. If you have trust and pleasure in your customers, as well as their respect, then you will generate more sales and you will have customers who stay with you over the long term.

There are, however, other ways of generating sales that use other emotions. For example, you might create scarcity by limiting an offer by time or number, or you might use a sales funnel where multiple purchases are available on an 'exclusive' basis. These sorts of sales techniques do work in the short term. They play on the anxiety that is created by making an offer seem about to slip through your fingers.

Unfortunately, when the same 'one-time' offer comes back up in the advertising a few months later, then people begin to get wise. It makes them doubt your future offers and it means they view future products with a degree of cynicism.

But your job is selling good feelings. When you use your why to motivate and engage your customers, they are already buying into the bigger picture. They know exactly why they're buying from you. You'll create a customer base that cares, and they'll be loyal to you because they *get* you and believe in your *why*.

So, skip the dirty tricks. Authenticity is part of the mix— and is so important!

A Clear Mission Statement

Your mission statement is a way of neatly communicating what your business does. It helps others and your own team understand what you do, and is a means to keep the business on track, as well as enabling development of your products within its parameters. It's a really useful tool that will help everyone who is in contact with your business *get* you. You should be able to communicate your mission statement in one short paragraph, maybe two. Put another way, if you present it to someone, then your clear, concise mission statement should take about half a minute to say out loud.

This is The Best You's mission statement:

The Best You is in the business of helping people achieve their dreams. We care, we listen to, and provide our customers with skills, tools, knowledge, wisdom, and experts to enhance and improve their lives. Ultimately we help people discover their true purpose.

Questions to answer in your mission statement:

Who is your company?

What does your company do?

What do you and your company believe in? What are its objectives? Why?

Who are your markets?

How do your customers benefit from doing business with you?

What specific challenge or challenges in the market do you offer solutions for?

How is your company different from all the others doing what you do?

Think about this. It will really help. Too many companies are created that have never explicitly worked out their core reasons for trading!

Understand the Numbers

As great as your idea can be and probably is, can you make the numbers add up? It's a mistake I have made several times in my life—not understanding if a business is viable. Look hard at the numbers. Work them out. At the end of the day, projects require funding. If you are working on a very tight budget to stay in business, it's a truism to say that you need to remember to bring in more money than you spend. You need strategies to make that work, and understanding the numbers will make clear where you need to change things.

If numbers are not your thing, get someone who loves them. This is absolutely vital.

Understand Business

I've come across so many people who are not interested in or prepared to learn the many different aspects of business. Although you don't have to master them all, having a clear understanding of how you can use social media to create awareness and build your brand, marketing, copywriting, selling, phone communication skills, how to create revenue streams are very important, not only to stay in business but to flourish and stand out.

Make business your study. Speak to people who have experience, read books, go to seminars. Get a mentor. Find out about all the different aspects of running a business so that you aren't suddenly surprised or caught out not knowing about one side of the business you should have done. There are plenty of books on the subject, and successful people are often willing to talk about their insights. Be curious. Seek to understand!

Understand Who Your Avatar Is, Your Customer

To make your business work well and to keep it directed towards your customers so you can work out what their needs are and how you can serve them, you need a picture of what your customer is like.

One way to do this is to create a kind of idealised virtual customer—to create, actually, an avatar or several avatars who typify who you understand your customer to be. They're kind of fictitious representations of customers, and by visualising and understanding them you get to think about them all the better.

As so much business is now done online, it takes some thinking about. After all, the days every customer walked in through the front door of your bricks-and-mortar shop or business are long gone.

You might want to consider your customer avatar while you're designing your business and your website. For example, visualising yourself into the lived experience of your customer will help you identify pinch points in your business. What you are looking for is a customer experience that is quick, easy, responsive, where they feel they have been understood and looked after. You want to avoid undue stress, disappointment and uncertainty. Your customer wants to feel satisfied.

Making your customer more real can be done by gathering basic information about your customers, so that you can visualise them and their experience with you. Gather data where you can, and once you have a sense of who is buying from you, think how you can help them further.

Ask yourself:

- What is your customer avatar's name?
- Male or female?
- Their age?
- What are their levels of qualification?

- What are they qualified in?

- What are their interests that drew them to you?

- Where do they work?

- What's their annual income?

- Where do they live?

Building resilience in business

I have been in business for the last 30 years. I have come up with all sorts of new ideas, and new businesses and, let me be clear, not all have worked. I believe that having a mission and a clear, slick brand does not necessarily provide or guarantee success.

You can feel very lonely running a business. It's not easy, you have to work very hard and put many hours in. I can't say I have loved every moment of my time running businesses. There have been highs and lows and some of the lows have been very low. But although it can be difficult, it can also be very rewarding. I love being in charge of my own destiny, I love creating something, I love the end result and the satisfaction I get from a job well done, when I deliver.

I love the Japanese proverb, *'fall down seven times, get up eight'.*

That has always been my thing. When I feel beaten, when I have had a bad day (and I have had my fair share!), I get back up. And when I do, I am actually more motivated and more driven.

It's also true that humans are creatures of habit. I have repeated the same mistakes many times but I try and make sure I learn from them. I keep fighting, I keep coming back.

* * *

'History is, strictly speaking, the study of questions; the study of answers belongs to anthropology and sociology'.

—W.H Auden

* * *

Chapter 6

THE WORLD

Dr Sylvia Earle is truly remarkable person, having dedicated her life to the protection of the world's oceans. A marine biologist, explorer, author and lecturer, Dr Earle was named by *Time* magazine as its first 'Hero for the Planet' in 1998, was the first female chief scientist for the US National Oceanic and Atmospheric Administrations and is part of the environmental group known as the Ocean Elders. She has said many inspiring things, and these quote below really hit home for me.

> *'You cannot care about what you do not know'*

and

> *'What we do in the next years will have an impact on the next 10,000 years'*

Giving a TED talk in 2009, Dr Earle said:

> *'Astronauts and aquanauts alike really appreciate the importance of air, food, water, temperature—all the things you need to stay alive in space or under the sea. I heard astronaut Joe Allen explain how he had to learn everything he could about his life support system and then do everything he could to take care of his life support system; and then he pointed to this [i.e.: the world around us] and he said, "Life support system." We need to learn everything we can about it and do everything we can to take care of it. Referring to the fact that this world, this planet is our and our children's and their children's life support system.'*

Dr Earle is clear that we shouldn't accept what is happening to the planet. Our life support system is in the worst danger we have ever known, and the fact is, we can't afford to sit back and do nothing.

This part of the book is, in my opinion, the most important part. It's the big picture. It's the part where you and your drives and motivation fit into the whole world. I said you should think big, after all, and if you're doing the best for yourself, then doing the best for the world is part of that.

So, in this section, my intention is to make you aware of some of what's happening around us. After all, as Dr Earle said, if you don't know, you can't care.

Many things in the world need addressing. I've gone for just a few—but the research is there for you to find out more. So, if I have left any subjects out that are close to your heart I apologise in advance. And maybe that's where your heart is telling you to put your attention, after all!

The Facts

Issues we must all take responsibility for:

1. Hunger

2. Slavery

3. War

4. Gender inequality

5. Racism

6. Extinction of wild life

7. Reducing plastic waste

8. Global Warming

1. Hunger

A shocking United Nations report* from 2015 gives the following horrific statistics about world hunger.

* 795 million people—or one in nine of the world's population—do not have enough to eat and thus do not have access to the nutrients and vitamins essential for proper development and health.

* 98 per cent of the world's undernourished people live in developing countries.

* In 2015, 800 million people went to bed hungry each night.

* The world's children are disproportionately affected by food and nutrition shortages.

* As of 2015, 90 million children under the age of five— one in seven worldwide—were underweight.

* Ninety per cent of the world's hungry children live in just two regions: Southern Asia and sub-Saharan Africa.

* Living with chronic hunger and malnutrition puts children at risk of dying from common colds and infection. Even if children do recover from these diseases, their recovery times are often delayed.

* Globally, 160 million children have inadequate height due to chronic hunger and malnutrition.

* 35 million people die of hunger every year.

*Source United Nations report http://www.un.org/millenniumgoals/2015_
MDG_Report/pdf/MDG%202015%20rev%20(July%201).pdf

What is worse, according to a report in the *Guardian*, food waste is extremely high. Annually, approximately one-third of all food produced for human consumption is wasted. That includes about 45 per cent of all fruit and vegetables, 35 per cent of fish and seafood, 30 per cent of cereals, 20 per cent of dairy products and 20 per cent of meat. It amounts to around 1.3 billion tonnes of food that is allowed to go to waste each year.

In the UK alone, 15 million tonnes of food are lost or wasted each year. Consumers throw away 4.2 million tonnes of edible food annually. Foods most often to be found in British bins are bread, vegetables, fruit and milk.

The Questions to ask yourself:

What can I do to address this?

What can I do to help?

What cause can I support?

How can I avoid wasting food?

How can I help get food to those who need it the most?

What charities or legacies can I support?

These questions are not going to have answers straight away. You may feel helpless in the face of the scale of the problem, and with such extraordinary statistics. But having the intention to work together with others of a similar mind, with a similar consciousness, can make a difference. We are all together on an increasingly small and increasingly interlinked world. Your success does not need to be at the expense of others. You can pay your success forward, to help those who are left behind. That is the next step of human consciousness.

2. Slavery

Slavery comes about by dehumanising people, removing them from being considered as having the special human qualities of independent thought and feelings for other people.

In Brené Brown's book, *Braving the Wilderness*, she talks about how dehumanisation occurs. In cases of conflict, she points out how most people find the idea of murder, torture and other human rights violations opposed to their moral code, provided they see the other person as included within their moral code. Brené describes how it's easy to see someone with a different political view as an 'asshole' when considered as part of the group they belong to, even though you happen to know personally members of the group whom you actually respect.

But the need to see the larger world, the bigger threat takes away individual positive traits. A narrative begins in which people are described as being outside of the normal moral codes you adhere to. The Nazis called the Jews *Untermenschen*, that is, subhumans. Slave owners also justified their brutal treatment of their slaves by considering them as livestock—that is, as animals. Once this new frame is created, then you are able to exclude groups from your moral view. After that, you can do anything you want to them.

The history of slavery is a long and cruel one. From the start of the 16th century to the 19th, slavery allowed Great Britain, the Netherlands and France to become leading world economies. More than 10 million people were sent to the Americas as slaves.

We in the West, look back on these times as ancient history. But they are not.

Brené's description of dehumanisation is going on right now. Indeed, she argues that in the modern world, we are even more susceptible to these dehumanising tendencies with the rise of social media and 24-hour news that simply reinforces what we have already been told.

For modern slavers, the same kinds of calculations are made as the ones their predecessors made. People will see slaves through the filter of dehumanisation that they have picked up and accepted as part of the dominant group. That is certainly the case with traditional slavery, in which society was told a convenient lie about slaves, which enabled them to ignore their suffering. But slavery is nowhere near as prevalent as it once was, right? We have gone beyond this. The world is a more civilised place than back then. . . Right?

The shocking truth about slavery is that, although it was abolished around 150 years ago in the USA, there are more people in slavery today than at any other time in world history.

Tens of millions of people are trapped in various forms of slavery throughout the world, right now. Research estimates that 40 million, I'll repeat that, 40 million people are enslaved worldwide. The revenue for traffickers from slavery is estimated to be around $150 billion annually. The work they are forced to carry out varies from forced labour, including child soldiers, to prostitution and being child brides in forced marriages, treated as goods.

214 / THE QUESTION

- Roughly 78 per cent of modern slavery involves labour slavery. It's not only the manual labour in fields, though it can include mining, logging, ranching, fishing and much more besides. Slavery can also be found in the service industries, where cleaners, gardeners and maids are forced to work under inhuman conditions for little or no pay.

- It is also estimated that 22 per cent of slaves are trapped in forced prostitution.

- Of all these slaves, about 26 per cent are children.

Is there anything more despicable than enslaving another human being? The fact is, there are enslaved people closer to you than you think.

A global charity called *A21* is doing vital work to raise awareness about slavery, as well as working to free modern-day slaves. A21 has a powerful slogan that I think applies equally to all the subjects in this chapter:

'*No one can do everything but everyone can do something*'. We must take action.

* * *

'Life's most persistent and urgent question is, 'what are you doing for others?"
—Martin Luther King

* * *

The Questions to ask yourself:

Was I aware of this modern world problem?

Is there someone I can help in this situation?

How can I help?

What charities or legacies can I support?

You can start by finding out more at A21 and other anti-slavery organisations.

3. War

There are several different ways to define what a war is, but a commonly quoted definition is that it is an *active conflict that has claimed more than 1000 lives.*

A figure quoted by the *New York Times* puts the prevalence of war in perspective. According to some reckonings, of the past 3400 years, humans have been entirely at peace for 268 of them. That's just 8 per cent of recorded history, less than one-twelfth.

In the 20th century alone, at least 108 million people were killed in wars. The total number of people killed in all wars throughout all of human history is estimated upto 1 billion.

Innocent civilians in the hundreds of thousands, if not millions, die annually because of war. Tens of millions have been displaced and are living in resettlement camps. How many are being murdered and tortured is impossible to say, but terrorism and human rights violations are going on every day.

When these wars are completely forgotten and ignored, each and every death is even more tragic.

Were you aware of this?

How much more will you be able to help when you have more influence and power?

Questions to ask yourself:

Is there something I can do?

Is there someone I know in a country at war or in this situation?

How can I help?

4. Gender Equality

To the modern eye, it almost seems unbelievable that it was so late in history before basic equal rights between men and women were recognised by law. It was not until 1975 in the UK that the Sex Discrimination Act was established to make it illegal to discriminate against women in employment, education and training.

It is worth stopping to consider for a moment that in Britain before the 1970s a woman could not get a credit card, report workplace sexual harassment, serve in combat or get a mortgage or a loan without a male guarantor.

That so much of the truly important legislation was only passed within the last 50 years is a sobering thought for those men who deny that women are not treated fairly. The fact is, the world is full of instances of inequality and women are treated, used and abused by people in positions of power or by selfish and abusive men. The #MeToo movement in 2018 has been a stark example of how far there is to go yet.

In the pursuit of allowing everyone to become the best they can be, it's vital that we resist deeply conservative cultures around the world that do not allow women to be educated, to take part in civil and political life, and to act, speak and think freely.

We should question all cultures and religions that allow women and young girls to be given or sold to men by arranged marriages, and those that embrace female genital mutilation.

Women's emancipation is an essential movement. We should not stop until the world has realised full equality between men and women.

This is by no means the end of the struggle for women's emancipation, with increasingly more steps made along the way, but with attitudes among men who grew up in a world in which women were traditionally seen as inferior still deeply entrenched in some quarters.

The Questions to ask yourself:

> If you are a woman and you are free and live in a free society, what are you doing to help those in need?
>
> If you are a man, do you fight for women's equality?
>
> How can you make your surroundings equal?

How are you educating your kids towards helping equal rights?

Do you and your friends stand up to bullies?

5. Racism

Racism is a complex issue and drives very strong emotions, and rightly so. The history of groups abusing other groups because of the colour of their skin or a belief about them has already been starkly shown in this book in the discussion on the history of slavery. Of course, African-American racism isn't the only type, but it is an area that creates extremely strong feelings, not least because the legacy of slavery can still be seen in America in the educational system, in the prison system and in social structures generally.

In Britain, too, and across Europe, racism has an incredibly complex history. The history of the various empires of Europe was inextricably linked with a racist view of the world. Other peoples were regarded as inferior by Europeans, and abused because of it.

Yet every continent has its racists: those people who have fallen into the trap of dehumanising others in order to be able to feel a grievance more strongly, or make a political point more easily.

Let's be clear what I'm talking about with the term 'racism'. It's a set of beliefs or series of actions that are marked out by discrimination or prejudice against a person or a group based on judgements about different biological and ethnic features. It might be a different coloured skin that causes the prejudice, or it could be other genetic features. More broadly and loosely using the term, it can also include feelings of hatred toward a particular culture rather than a 'race' (the term 'race' is not recognised in modern scientific terms). So, it might discriminate against a religion, a nationality, a language and so on.

Although racism is strongly condemned by many governments and intergovernmental bodies, institutionalised racial inequality and discrimination are still widespread and can include not only discrimination, but also prejudice, verbal and physical assault.

State-sanctioned racism includes such phenomena as segregation, slavery, genocide, inequality, police brutality to particular ethnic/cultural groups. Examples of it at its worst include the transatlantic slave trade, European imperialism, US segregation, apartheid and Nazism.

Racism affects everybody because it breeds mistrust and suspicion. These in turn breed fear and hatred. There has been a general idea since World War II that the world is becoming more open and less fearful, with greater trade and travel opening up new cultures and borders. But in the last 10 years or so, there has been an increase in racism in what we think of as 'enlightened' countries.

Although international consensus evolved in the 20th century so that formerly accepted attitudes towards prejudice have been roundly rejected, with racism widely recognised as a crime, nevertheless racist attitudes persist. States, governments, private enterprises and individuals are all to blame.

Racism is a complex problem with countless minutiae and gradations. Anywhere one group is treated differently or unjustly, there is racism. And racism holds people back. It stops them being who they really are for fear of judgement and for lack of support. It encourages a mindset in some of its victims that they are never going to get on in life, that they are destined never to succeed. In some it breeds resentment and anger towards their oppressors. Racists themselves fear an idea of people they themselves have created or have been influenced into believing. And the confirmation bias in showing that people from some cultures do bad things only seeks to entrench views. At the same time, it's vital to recognise that there are cultural differences, which mean that some groups may indeed treat their women or children worse than others. If you have a mind to enable others to prevent abuse of power wherever it lies, then make that ideal your guiding light. Through education one can build empathy, understand how others feel—and rather than have prejudice, meet each person and work out who they are on their own terms.

The Questions to ask yourself:

Am I aware of situations of social injustice?

Am I non-judgemental?

How can I educate my children, family and those close to me?

Is the company I work for open to other cultures and ways of thinking?

6. Extinction of Wildlife

Humankind is the most successful species the world has ever seen. Think about that word *success* again. Do you remember what I said about having the right kind of success? About not being successful at the expense of those around you? The same can be said of humankind and its place in the world. It seems quite a strange idea, to call the degradation of our home and the extinction of countless animals that we share the planet with a success. Yet that is exactly what our success has meant. That is what I have been arguing for throughout this book—the idea of success as being wider than just about you.

A report from 2014 published in the *Guardian* discussed how hard our impact has been on the species we share the planet with. It revealed that the number of wild animals on Earth has halved in the past 40 years. Humans, it reports, are killing and destroying creatures on land, in rivers and in the seas for food, through pollution or through destruction of their habitats.

The analysis was performed by scientists at WWF and the Zoological Society of London. Professor Ken Norris, the Zoological Society's director of science, made the following comparison:

> 'If half the animals died in London Zoo next week, it would be front page news. But that is happening in the great outdoors. This damage is not inevitable but a consequence of the way we choose to live.'

This isn't only being sentimental about animals. As Dr Sylvia Earle pointed out, our planet is our life support system. That so many animals are dying out is a sign that the entity that provides our food, water and air is under unprecedented strain. The consequences for humanity are potentially dire.

Marine animal populations have also fallen by 40 per cent overall, and if ecosystems throughout the seas are stressed too far, then we may find our seas fished out. The problem is unwise and unchecked consumption. As the *Guardian* reports, as poorer countries often supply goods and food to wealthier countries, rich countries are outsourcing environmental decline to poorer ones.

The result is that the world is operating at unsustainable levels of consumption, with calculations that, at current levels, today's average rate of consumption requires 1.5 Earths to sustain it. UK consumption, were it the same throughout the whole world, would require 2.5 Earths. US consumption would require 4.

But things can be done to stabilise and reverse this. Some countries are showing that animal life can be saved, if the right will is put to it. Intensive conservation efforts with tigers in Nepal have turned the population decline around. And animals are not just things to save; the health of species is an indicator of the health of the world's ecosystem. It's vital that we get behind it.

The report concludes:

> 'We all—politicians, businesses and people—have an interest, and a responsibility, to act to ensure we protect what we all value: a healthy future for both people and nature.'

Shocking numbers:

- 99 per cent of currently threatened species are at risk due to human activity.

- The current extinction rate is estimated by experts to be between 1000 and 10,000 times higher than the natural extinction rate.

- Experts say humans are creating the sixth great extinction.

- WWF estimate that we could be losing as many as 100,000 species a year.

- Elephant populations have dropped by 62 per cent over the last decade.

- Poachers hunting for ivory, meat and body parts kill an estimated 100 African elephants A DAY.

- Only 400,000 African elephants remain.

- 30 per cent of Africa's savannah elephants were wiped out by poachers between 2007 and 2014.

- More than 6000 rhinos were shot and butchered *for their horns* in South Africa during a 10-year period starting in 2007.

- In the final four years of that period, a thousand were killed every year.

Some species we have lost:

- Spix macau

- Javan tiger

- West African black tiger

- Pyrenean ibex

- Golden toad

- Baiji dolphin

- Zanzibar leopard

The illegal wildlife trade is estimated at between $10 and $20 billion a year, and is linked to organised crime. It harms endangered wildlife, fuels conflicts, feeds corruption and undermines poverty eradication efforts.

Questions to ask yourself:

What can I do?

What will I do?

Do I care enough to make a difference?

Are there any charities or legacies I can help or support?

7. Plastic Waste

One increasingly serious problem facing the modern world is plastics pollution. The problem has been building up for the last 70 years or so, although plastics themselves have been around for far longer than that.

The first modern plastic, Parkesine, was invented in 1856 by Alexander Parkes, a chemist in Birmingham, UK. Over the following century, advances were made in plastic manufacture, including the creation of Bakelite and polystyrene, mass production of PVC, polyethylene, polypropylene and many more substances. Now, plastics have proliferated in both type and use, and their cheapness and disposability have led to the problem of mass usage without anyone thinking about how to actually dispose of them safely.

Because some plastics can take up to 1000 years to biodegrade, they are simply hanging around in the environment. As they age, they don't fully decompose, but break into smaller and smaller parts until they are microscopic. This has created a whole new problem for humanity to face—that of microplastics pollution. In the sea, microplastics are getting into the food chain and poisoning wildlife, as was highlighted by a BBC documentary, *Blue Planet*, which showed the slow death of a whale calf in the oceans due to plastics poisoning. A 2017 study reported by *Time* magazine revealed that on average, 83 per cent of all the world's tap water is contaminated with plastic microfibres. In Europe an average of 72 per cent of tap water samples were contaminated. In the USA, it was 94 per cent.

It's estimated that 50 per cent of all plastics are used in single-use items, but plastics aren't just found in obvious throw-away items such as packaging and disposable items like pens and razors.

Plastics are found in paint, in clothing and in countless consumer goods. Billions of miles of electric cabling are insulated with plastic, while pipework is made from it; it is found in take-away food containers and building materials, in car tyres and countless other places. Plastics pollution has now reached record levels in the once-pristine Arctic. It's found all over the Earth, in soil, air and water.

Annually, in excess of 8 million tonnes of plastic are dumped into our seas. 300 million tonnes of plastic now litter the oceans, and though much of it can be seen floating on the surface, even the deepest trenches are being affected.

Yet plastic in itself doesn't have to be the enemy—it is, after all, a valuable resource. How we deal with it, however, does need to change in a major way.

* * *

> 'No water, no life. No blue, no green.'
> —Dr Sylvia Earle

* * *

Some plastics statistics (courtesy of plasticoceans.org):

- 40 per cent of total plastics produced are used in packaging.

- An estimated 500 billion plastic bags are used each year. That's over a million bags per minute.

- Each plastic bag is actually used on average for just 15 minutes.

- The last ten years has seen more plastics produced than through the whole of the 20th century.

Beverage Bottles Alone

- 100.7 billion plastic beverage bottles were sold in the USA alone in 2014. That's 315 bottles per person.

- 57 per cent of those units were plastic water bottles: 57.3 billion sold in 2014. This is up from 3.8 billion plastic water bottles sold in 1996, the earliest year for available data.

- The process of producing bottled water requires around six times as much water per bottle as there is in the container.

- 14 per cent of all litter comes from beverage containers. When caps and labels are considered, the number is higher.

And What's More

- The USA alone uses 500 million plastic straws EACH DAY. Laid end to end, they would stretch around the circumference of the Earth two and a half times. Every day. . .

- Because they are too small to be recycled they are thrown away and often end up in the sea. Plastic straws are major polluters and can be harmful to animals.

The good news is that governments around the world are now banning the use of plastic and measures are starting to come into place. Yet we have created a massive problem for future generations and it requires <u>everyone's</u> attention.

The Questions to ask yourself:

Do I care enough to do something?

How am I helping?

What can I do?

Where can I find out more?

Am I educating my kids?

Who can I support?

8. *Global Warming*

I find it bewildering that the argument about global warming is even happening. A study found that 97 per cent of actively published climate scientists agree that man-made global warming is real. There is not really a strong debate to be had. If it weren't for a few maverick climate scientists who are either misunderstanding the data or are wilfully misleading the public, the debate would be long over. However, there is too much vested interest that doesn't want to confront the idea of change and wants to protect its investments in the oil industry. It really is as simple as that.

For those people who aren't experts, then it is a bewildering choice to make. A general emotion of distrusting scientists who don't tell you what you want to hear has been growing in the world, along with a reactionary attitude that rebels against reasoned argument. Remember what I said before about how emotions sway decisions? In the case of man-made climate change, people's emotions are being fired up and directed, rather than reason being used. Unfortunately, this isn't about getting someone to buy a product you produce or invest in your company. It's about denying the harm human beings are doing to the planet, and using emotions to keep yourself comfortable by avoiding facing up to hard truths. But this is only going to make things harder for everyone. My advice to climate change deniers is, for the love of your kids and their kids, read more, research, wake up and act. Even if there is the slimmest chance that the vast majority of climate change scientists are right (and they are) then you cannot afford to risk your children's future to feed your sense of identity, indignation or political bias. Get beyond it.

Think for a moment. Do you really believe that the huge population of the Earth, with its use of more and more resources—so much more than 50, 100, or 200 years ago— does not have an impact on the planet? Human beings are constantly destroying forests, building more cars and roads, creating more pollution. Is it such a huge step to think that this might be affecting the way the atmosphere behaves? Do you really think that the vast proliferation in electrical goods, cars, plastics, household goods, boats—everything that humanity manufactures—has no effect on the world it is made from? Really? How is that even possible?

Climate scientist John Cook released a fascinating report that shows how the amount of heat being built up in the Earth due to human activity is equivalent to 4 Hiroshima bombs every second, or put another way, somewhere around 350,000 Hiroshima bombs every day.

This is having its effect. As the globe warms, warmer air is holding more water over the desert regions of the world, with some of them now starting to show early signs of sprouting into life. On the other side of the equation, recent studies have shown that the Amazon rainforest could be seriously affected by climate change and man-made emissions, with the potential to turn it into desert in a few short years if drought were to set in. This would release a huge amount of stored carbon into the atmosphere as the trees died and broke down, and would accelerate climate change drastically.

CO_2 levels in the atmosphere have increased by 34 per cent since the 17th century. This is being absorbed by the sea, which is becoming increasingly acidic. Already, shellfish and corals are starting to show signs of weakening and dying due to increased sea acidity. The Great Barrier Reef is going through an ecological shock, with corals dying off at an extraordinary rate due to sea acidification. Estimates state that the acidity of the world's oceans since the beginning of the Industrial Revolution has increased by approximately 30 per cent.

Between the years 1961 and 1997, the world's glaciers lost 890 cubic miles of ice. As the northern ice cap melts due to rising temperatures, sea levels are also beginning to rise. Low lying land across the world is being swallowed up by the sea. A one-metre rise would be enough to displace over 100 million people. Meanwhile, for the first time, regular freight ships are able to travel through the Northwest Passage above North America.

27 per cent of all the world's carbon emissions comes from the USA. No wonder people don't want to face up to the truth—it would mean huge changes in their way of life. The chief cause of carbon emissions is from cars, of which there are expected to be over a billion by 2030 and over two billion by 2050.

And kudos to some inspiring men—to Al Gore and his *Global Reality Project* and all the amazing work he has done to create awareness of global warming. Also to Leonardo DiCaprio's amazing documentary *Before The Flood*.

That said, we are all responsible and those in power have to take action. There are some signs of things going in the right direction, and on 22 April 2016 the Paris Agreement was signed by 195 out of 196 of the world's countries, with only North Korea declining to sign. The Agreement set targets for the reduction of carbon and aims to limit global warming to between 1 and 2 degrees centigrade. In 2017, the USA also dropped out of the agreement, leaving other countries to push on and take the lead. France has already announced its intention to phase out all petrol and diesel cars by 2040, and stop burning coal for power production by 2022. So, while former leaders in the world become less relevant, others see the opportunities for renewal and change that dealing with climate change brings. That is one of the examples about how adapting to change keeps you ahead.

My first question is: how are people and some world leaders denying the facts?

Questions to ask yourself:

So the question, here and now, is what am I doing?

How am I helping?

Understanding the concept 'No one can do everything but everyone can do something', how can I contribute at home?

In how I travel?

At work? Or in the world?

How committed am I to help?

Inspirers—Leaders and Influencers

One thing I've really learned over my time working in personal development is how inspiring the lives of others can be in helping to shape your story. So, as we come to the end of the book, I want to review the life and stories of some amazing human beings. These are people who have changed the world for the better and made an extraordinary impact. Of course, there are possibly millions of people we could feature, but here I will look at just a few from different parts of the world, and really enjoy their achievements.

Martin Luther King Jr was born in 1929, the son and grandson of pastors at the Ebenezer Baptist Church, Atlanta, where King also later became co-pastor. He went on to become a leader in the civil rights movement as a member of the National Association for the Advancement of

Coloured People. He led the first great nonviolent protest against segregation on buses, and fought for freedom and equality for black people. During protests, he was arrested, his home was bombed, he was subjected to personal abuse. In an 11-year period between 1957 and 1968, King went on to speak and fight for the rights of African Americans, using the nonviolent techniques employed by Gandhi. He travelled over six million miles and spoke over 2500 times, appearing wherever there was injustice, protest, and action. He was arrested more than 20 times and assaulted at least four times; he was awarded five honorary degrees; was named Man of the Year by *Time* magazine in 1963; and became not only the symbolic leader of African-Americans but also a world figure. He was the youngest man to receive the Nobel Peace Prize. He was assassinated in 1968 in Tennessee, where he was due to lead a protest march. His legacy, as well as his famous 'I have a dream' speech, resounds through history.

Franklin D. Roosevelt led the United States through the Great Depression and World War II. Stricken with polio in 1921 at the age of 39, Roosevelt spent much of his adult life in a wheelchair. A whole generation of Americans grew up knowing no other president, as FDR served an unprecedented four terms in office. Roosevelt's social programs reinvented the role of government in Americans' lives, while his presidency during World War II established the United States' leadership on the world stage.

Muhammad Ali is one of the great names of modern sporting history, and a central figure in the Civil Rights movement in the USA. Although he was remembered with deep

234 / THE QUESTION

fondness at the end of his life by adoring fans, this wasn't always the case. In earlier years, during the 1960s, he had won gold at the Olympics for boxing, but was still insulted in his town, and even barred from restaurants because of the colour of his skin. Ali refused to fight in the Vietnam War, for which he was stripped of his medals, briefly jailed and reviled by many. Yet he went on to become a legend of the modern world, admired and loved by his country.

Victor Frankl was an Austrian psychiatrist and psychotherapist born in 1905, who died in 1997. Frankl created a psychological approach called logotherapy, which puts forward the idea that the primary drive for survival is meaning. He developed his views while being interned in Nazi concentration camps in Word War II, where he observed that those who had some meaning in their lives were more likely to survive. He is largely regarded as offering the third form of psychotherapy, after Freudianism and Jungianism, and his work is a powerful take on what it is to have meaning in life.

Jean-Dominique Bauby wrote the number one best-selling *Diving Bell and The Butterfly*, which was adapted into a multiple award-winning movie. His story is a tragic one and also one of extreme endurance. After suffering a massive stroke at the age of 43, he woke up to find himself completely paralysed and only able to blink. Bauby, despite this severe paralysis, wrote his book, using a system called partner-assisted scanning, in which he blinked his way through the alphabet in order to create the right word. He composed the entire book in his head, dictating it one letter at a time. Two days after his book was published in

1997, Bauby was suddenly struck with pneumonia and died. His book is a lasting epitaph to his imagination and determination.

Ludwig van Beethoven is considered one of the world's greatest classical composers. Born in 1770 in Germany, Beethoven grew up with an alcoholic father, whom he escaped from in his music. He had an extraordinary talent for writing on the piano and began composing at the age of 12. His work became famous, but in 1801 he began to lose his hearing. He continued to compose, even after he went completely deaf, using his memory for the sounds and the vibrations transmitted through his piano to his legs to sense the notes. He did not allow his deafness to beat him, but instead went on to become an even more prolific composer, and he never actually heard much of his most famous music, such as the 'Moonlight' sonata, the 'Pathetique' and his incredible 9th symphony.

Jesse Owens experienced racial discrimination in his native country, the USA, but became a global hero when he competed in the 1936 Berlin Olympics. By winning Olympic gold in the 100 m, Owens laid bare the lies at the heart of Hitler's ideas of Aryan superiority, and is a hero for anyone who cares about equal rights for all people.

Malala Yousafzai is the Pakistani schoolgirl who was shot in the head by the Taliban for daring to suggest that girls should have a right to education. Rushed to Europe for life-saving treatment, she survived and went on to become a prominent campaigner for human rights, women's rights and the right to education.

Marina Silva is a Brazilian environmentalist who, as a young woman, conquered five battles against malaria, grew up in conditions of poverty and did not learn to read until she was a teenager. Her parents were rubber tappers and she was one of eleven children, three of whom died while young. Silva became a political activist while supporting rubber tappers and went on to become Brazil's youngest Senator ever at the age of 36. She remains an environmental activist in Brazil and worldwide, and is currently a member of the United Nations Secretary-General's MDG Advocacy Group.

Prime Minister Narendra Modi of India had extremely humble beginnings in Northern India in Vadnagar, one of six. He used to go to work in his father's tea shop before school each day. As a member of the Modh-Ghanchi caste in India, which is one of the Other Backward Classes (OBCs) or disadvantaged castes, he faced prejudice and disadvantage. He is now listed as the 13th most influential person in the world by *Forbes* magazine.

Helen Keller was born both deaf and blind, but went on to learn how to write, becoming a world-renowned champion of social issues and helping to improve the welfare of deaf people.

Jessica Cox was born without any arms, but went on to graduate in psychology, write, type, drive a car, brush her hair and talk on her phone by using her feet. She is a double black belt in Taekwondo, can drive on a no-restrictions licence and, perhaps her most famous achievement, is a qualified pilot—becoming the world's first pilot with no arms.

These figures above, some more famous and well-known than others, are a varied and eclectic mix. They are just a handful of the extraordinary, inspirational people from whom it's possible to learn great lessons in life. From FDR's undaunted determination, through Martin Luther King's passion and sense of deep justice and Malala Yousafzai's clear sense of what's right, there is so much to learn. The brilliance of a composer like Beethoven and the creative genius of Walt Disney are equally wonderful characters to be enjoyed, learned from and modelled.

Of course, the world has many, many inspiring people beyond these few above. There are those who led the way in the past and those who continue to do so now, those who have clear knowledge of how the world needs to change and those who know how to make it happen, who can see what we need to take care of, what needs addressing. There are heroes around us all the time, who do amazing things but won't be mentioned in encyclopaedias and obituaries—those who make a difference in their everyday lives. Who are those for you? Who are your big heroes, and who are your everyday heroes? Learn from them.

Wealth Redistribution

One of the things I've really come to admire is how people in positions of power and wealth, who don't need to do anything for others, are working to make the world a better place and address major challenges. They include film stars, politicians and business leaders.

Wealth inequality has been growing at an alarming rate over the last few decades. A 2017 report by Oxfam revealed that the wealth of the 3.6 billion poorest people in the world is equivalent to the wealth of just eight men. That means that eight men have the same wealth as half of the entire world put together. The report, *An Economy For The 99 Percent*, shows how much wider the gap between rich and poor has become than most people imagined. It reveals the scale of tax avoidance and evasion by those wealthy enough to find ways to keep their money hidden from the taxman. At the same time, the super-rich are using their influence to drive down wages and influence politics, meaning that the world's economies stop working for everyone but favour the few who are already extremely rich.

The figures are sobering. One in ten people survive on less than $2 a day. Hundreds of millions are trapped in a cycle of poverty due to lack of opportunities, corruption and low education. It's fracturing societies and means that people all over the world are being left behind with stagnating wages, while corporate bosses take home obscene amounts of money.

The richest people in the world are accumulating wealth at such an astonishing rate, the report notes, that the first trillionaire could be created in just 25 years. To make sense of such an extraordinary figure, you would need to spend $1 million every day over a period of 2738 years to spend $1 trillion.

The super-wealthy enjoy advantages with investments that are closed to ordinary investors, and their wealth is often either inherited or might be made in sectors prone to corruption. Meanwhile, the discontent at how little wealth is 'trickling down' to the rest of the populace has been blamed for the discontent of voters across the world, who voted for far right leaders with extreme policies, who appear to promise change, but will deliver no such thing.

Solutions are available if governments work together to end the extreme concentration of wealth in the hands of a few by increasing taxes and supporting opportunities for the world's poorest people. Only this way can the world improve.

And among some enlightened wealthy people, there is agreement. For example, there is a growing interest in philanthropy among Silicon Valley's billionaires. Bill Gates, Warren Buffett and Mark Zuckerberg are at the vanguard of this new consciousness—seeking to give away much of their fortunes before they die.

They are right. Ignoring the problems and the challenges of the world is no longer an option. To do so will create more problems, more suffering and more instability in the years to come, in which the world is already under stress from over-consumption.

All of these problems—the environment, poverty, education and wealth—are deeply connected and are part of the litany of injustices we see in the world. There is a saying that, as you get older, you begin to become more selfish. I have to say, this is not always true. For me, I admit my consciousness about world problems has come late in life. I will be honest: in the past, I've always looked from a distance at volunteers and philanthropists. It's not been something on my radar. I suppose, like many, I simply never understood—or simply felt it wasn't my concern.

But my work in the personal development world has made me focus far more on people and their suffering than before. There is no *right time* or *right age* to become environmentally and globally responsible and aware. What happens is, as you become increasingly aware of the problems and ignorance strips away, an emotional response comes from within that seeks to answer the questions each new revelation forces you to ask.

For me, and I hope for you, the answers that come back will show that you are ready to help. That way we can help others out of poverty and suffering so we can all become the best we can be.

Things need to change. The Questions to ask yourself:

> Am I aware of this?
>
> Do I care?
>
> Is this a cause worthy of me?
>
> What can I do to make a difference?
>
> How can I help?
>
> What can you I do?
>
> When?

YOUR Responsibility—OUR Responsibility

Of course, injustice has been around since the beginning of time. Humanity has moved forward and achieved so many great things, but we still have so much more to accomplish.

I hope you will become passionate about the things that need to change, too. As you know, my goal is that you come to an understanding that the best version of yourself means that you want to work with others to make the world a better version of itself too.

Once we are able to find peace within ourselves, and we become at ease with our soul, with our loved ones, with our past and our present, we can go on to dedicate our lives to becoming 'unselfish' and ultimately making the world an amazing and inspiring place.

Have you ever spoken to a volunteer, those amazing individuals who give up their free time or are dedicating their lives to injustice? With many, you will see the passion in their eyes, the love, the hope, the fulfilment they have because they are doing something useful and trying to make a difference.

We have to hope we leave this planet in a better place than we found it. We are merely custodians of the Earth and must look after it for future generations.

How can we address so many issues mankind must deal with?

It all comes back to the educational revolution. Literacy around the world is essential, a lifeline that means people feel connected and have the personal agency to learn about the world. Rather than spreading distrust and misinformation as many do, I think it's vital to offer something different. To offer opportunity to others, so they can grasp it and use it to make their lives better. That's the sort of education I'm talking about. The curriculum has to be adapted to the new world we live in; many of the curriculums do not cover the essential things that need addressing in this 21st century that we live in.

I want to make that revolution happen.

This book, in many ways, is my manifesto.

Now, it's time for you to write yours.

Think about it.

In this book we have gone through history, what it takes to succeed, the heroes who came before us, and those now leading the way. We've looked at the power of Resilience, Revolution and Reinvention.

What I would like you to do now is to STOP and GO.

STOP lying to yourself

STOP looking for excuses

STOP blaming others

STOP ignoring what you need to do

STOP ignoring the facts

STOP not contributing

STOP not helping

STOP not making a difference

GO and start making positive changes, NOW!

I think I have mentioned previously when writing about Brené Brown's work and the false creation of excluded groups, that really there is no 'they'!

You are 'they'. I am 'they'. We all are.

These are my final thoughts my friend, *mi amig@*.

I don't have all the answers—far from it. I am far from perfect. I am only human, I make mistakes and when I do they are big ones and having changed my life several times, and being who I am as founder of The Best You, I am continually asking myself 'am I the best version I can be'?

I often also review the words I share with others.

'Change is good'

'Break your limiting beliefs'

'What else am I capable of doing?'

'Who can I STILL become?'

'Am I holding back trying to keep others happy'?

So in this part of my life I have decided to be selfish, but not in the way I have spoken of before. I have decided to take care of myself, follow my dreams, my hopes because my sense of self includes helping others. *That* kind of selfishness is what I mean. Of course, some people may not understand my journey. So in my next book and in the next chapter of my life, I will be exploring 'selfish development' in both its positive and negative aspects. I hope you will join me.

To end the book, my son Lucci pointed this last quote out to me on a YouTube link, and I feel it sums up the journey we are on. In his Oscar Award acceptance speech, actor Matthew McConaughey shared his own manifesto:

> '*There are three things I need each day. A trilogy that gives me focus, keeps me questioning and drives me on to make the best decisions for me and those around me. The first is I need something to look up to, the second is something to look forward to, and the last is something to chase.*

> '*When I was 15 years old, I had a very important person in my life come to me and say "who's your hero?" And I said, "I don't know, I gotta think about that. Give me a couple of weeks." I come back two weeks later, this person comes up and says "who's your hero?" I said, "I thought about it. You know who it is? It's me in 10 years." So I turned 25. Ten years later, that same person comes to me and says, "So, are you a hero?" And I was like, "not even close. No, no, no." She said, "Why?" I said, "Because my hero's me at 35." So you see every day, every week, every month and every year of my life, my hero's always 10 years away. I'm never gonna be my hero. I'm not gonna attain that. I know I'm not, and that's just fine with me because that keeps me with somebody to keep on chasing.*'

So be your own hero! Whatever you do, don't *be a time-waster*. Be your own hero. Life's too short!

And my final words for you are: What are your Questions? Ask yourself daily.

The End

Index

nature deficit disorder 117
Nazism 10, 212
Neill, Michael xx
Netflix 5
Neuro-Linguistic Programming
viii, xviii, 136–7
Never Give Up approach 58
New Three Rs 66–7
Newcomen, Thomas 86
Nietzsche, Friedrich 132
NLP Life Training viii
Norris, Ken 221
numbers, understanding 201–2

obesity 165
Ocean Elders 208
oil companies 22
optimism 10, 34, 148
Owens, Jesse 235

Palmer, Parker 155
parents 167–8
Paris Agreement (2016) 231
Parkes, Alexander 224
partner-assisted scanning 234
passion 60–1
personal true purpose 152–3
philanthropy 239
phobias 137, 139
physical health 79, 140, 148,
163–5
Picasso 101
Pilates 121
planning ahead 98
plastic waste 10, 22, 224–8
bottles 227
population, human 2, 7–8
poverty 83
Proctor, Bob xx
professional life 185–8
psychotherapy 234
PTSD 122
purpose 154–9
definition of 154
finding out your 156
personal true 152–3

quality of questions you ask yourself 27, 30

racism 218–20
Reaction Engines 5
reframing 80, 97–8, 99
reinvention 66, 67, 99–100, 104–5,
106–12, 148
religious mind 8
research 188–90
resilience 66, 67, 68–70, 73–6,
148, 204–5
seven key traits 79–81
studies in 71–3
respect 199
responsibility 43, 94–5, 240–4
revolution 66, 67, 81–99, 148
agricultural 82–5
Cultural Revolution (China) 9
educational 92–5
Industrial Revolution 5, 85–7
information 88–91
life 96–9
Robbins, Tony xx, 52, 167, 192
'I am not your Guru' 94
Robert the Bruce 68
Rocky 106
Rohn, Jim xx
Roman Empire 15
Roosevelt, Franklin D. 233, 237
Rowling, J.K. 72, 103
*Harry Potter and the
Philosopher's Stone* 103
ruts 106–7

sacrifice 8
sales funnel 199
Sanders, Colonel 194
satisfaction 56
Savage, Roz xiv, 182
Schwartz, Dr Kevin xx
Scotland: Agricultural Revolution 84
sea voyagers, historical 12–13
Secret, The (film) 65, 93, 143
self esteem, lack of 137
self-help 46
self-hypnosis 139
selfish development ix
self-motivated 64
self-reliance 45, 64
sense of destiny 81
Sex Discrimination Act
(1975) (UK) 216